# PRAISE FO

# WHAT WHITE PARENTS SHOULD KNOW
# ABOUT TRANSRACIAL ADOPTION

"Melissa Guida-Richards offers a generous summary of the multi-faceted and often-controversial practice of transracial adoption. Part confession, part guide, and part intellectual invitation, Guida-Richards offers expertise with patience and wit. This is a book of experiential knowledge from a transracially adopted person who has thought deeply about the subject. A book that is a true gift to those with enough courage to face it and themselves."

—Jenny Heijun Wills, author of *Older Sister.*
*Not Necessarily Related.*

"Guida-Richards provides a powerful and honest look at some of the most important topics in transracial adoption—topics that have historically all too often been avoided in conversations not only between adoptive parents, but between adoptive parents and their transracially adopted child: white saviorism, white privilege, racial identity, and much more. This should be on the mandatory reading and education list for ALL prospective adoptive parents."

—Christine Heimann, founder of Adoptee
Bridge, a nonprofit providing post-adoption
support for transracial adoptees and their
families

"Melissa Guida-Richards lays bare a painful truth: That loss is central to adoption. For those who are adopted transracially and transnationally, the disappearance of culture, familiarity, and language carry added complexity. With grace and sensitivity, Guida-Richards offers clear, insightful guidance for adoptive parents to help their sons and daughters navigate the isolation, racism, and longing they inevitably feel."

—Gabrielle Glaser, author of *American Baby*

"I'm an adoptive parent, I consult hopeful adoptive parents in their adoption journey, and I'm an avid adoption book enthusiast. This book is the most comprehensive, relevant, and recommended book to anyone connected and wanting to do better in adoption."

—Paige Knipfer, owner of Love Grown Adoption Consulting

"*What White Parents Should Know about Transracial Adoption* tackles the most necessary yet overlooked intricacies of adoption, refusing to gloss over the realities that children of color face. Guida-Richards has delivered a culturally relevant must-read for parents to advance their anti-racism education and to become strong advocates for their children."

—Kira Omans, actor, model, advocate, and transracial adoptee

# WHAT WHITE PARENTS SHOULD KNOW ABOUT TRANSRACIAL ADOPTION

## AN ADOPTEE'S PERSPECTIVE ON ITS HISTORY, NUANCES, AND PRACTICES

### MELISSA GUIDA-RICHARDS

#### FOREWORD BY PAULA GUIDA

North Atlantic Books
Berkeley, California

Published by
North Atlantic Books              Cover art © gettyimages.com/chrupka
Huichin, unceded Ohlone land      Cover design by Jasmine Hromjak
aka Berkeley, California

Book design by Happenstance Type-O-Rama
Printed in the United States of America

*What White Parents Should Know about Transracial Adoption: An Adoptee's Perspective on Its History, Nuances, and Practices* is sponsored and published by North Atlantic Books, an educational nonprofit based in the unceded Ohlone land Huichin (aka Berkeley, CA) that collaborates with partners to develop cross-cultural perspectives; nurture holistic views of art, science, the humanities, and healing; and seed personal and global transformation by publishing work on the relationship of body, spirit, and nature.

North Atlantic Books' publications are distributed to the US trade and internationally by Penguin Random House Publishers Services. For further information, visit our website at www.northatlanticbooks.com.

Library of Congress Cataloging-in-Publication Data
Names: Guida-Richards, Melissa, 1993– author.
Title: What white parents should know about transracial adoption : an
    adoptee's perspective on its history, nuances, and practices / Melissa
    Guida-Richards.
Description: Berkeley, CA : North Atlantic Books, [2021] | Includes
    bibliographical references and index. | Summary: "A guide for white
    parents of transracially or transnationally adopted children"— Provided
    by publisher.
Identifiers: LCCN 2021019827 (print) | LCCN 2021019828 (ebook) | ISBN
    9781623175825 (trade paperback) | ISBN 9781623175832 (ebook)
Subjects: LCSH: Interracial adoption. | Intercountry adoption. | Adoptive
    parents. | Adopted children—Psychology. | Ethnicity in children. | Race
    awareness.
Classification: LCC HV875.6 .G85 2021  (print) | LCC HV875.6  (ebook) | DDC
    362.734089—dc23
LC record available at https://lccn.loc.gov/2021019827
LC ebook record available at https://lccn.loc.gov/2021019828

2 3 4 5 6 7 8 9 KPC 26 25 24 23 22 21

North Atlantic Books is committed to the protection of our environment. We print on recycled paper whenever possible and partner with printers who strive to use environmentally responsible practices.

*For adoptive parents like mine,*
*who just need a little extra*
*help to do the work*

# CONTENTS

# FOREWORD

My name is Paula, and I was born in Portugal in a little town named Ovar where I was raised until I was nine. I grew up very poor and lived in a small three-room house with my parents, younger sisters, and grandma. In 1967, my maternal grandfather made arrangements for us to come to the United States to have a better life. We came at the end of 1969, went to school, and by the age of twelve, I was helping out my parents by washing dishes in a restaurant. By 1976, at the age of sixteen, I had met the love of my life who would later be my husband—his name was Rocky.

Being raised in a conservative family, I was not permitted to date at sixteen. It was rough waters when I told my dad that not only did I have a boyfriend, but that my boyfriend wanted to meet him. My dad decided to give Rocky a chance, but we were only allowed to see one another with a chaperone. By 1979, we were married. Over the next twelve years, we traveled and had a wonderful life, but we knew that something was missing. In 1990, my husband and I found a beautiful new colonial home in Fishkill, New York, where we knew we wanted to raise our children.

Unfortunately, years went by and we were not able to conceive. The attorney that did the closing on our house had mentioned adoption—she had adopted her oldest son through an agency and was very happy with them. By the time we met her,

her son was already well on the way to becoming an attorney himself. She gave us the information so we could get in touch with the adoption lawyer she used, and we were able to find out more about the process.

At that point in time, my husband and I did not want to know the cause of our infertility. In my heart of hearts, I've always thought that if I couldn't have biological children, the one thing I wanted to do was adopt and give a child the love, the home, and everything else they needed. We told the agency and lawyer that we were seeking an infant that would resemble us and, lo and behold, six months later we got a phone call letting us know about a child. We were sent a small little picture and vitals of a baby girl—as soon as we saw the picture, Rocky and I fell in love. We said yes immediately, without hesitation. About three months later, after a lot of paperwork and formalities, Rocky and I traveled to Colombia to meet her for the first time.

We did more paperwork processing in Colombia, came home, and several weeks later after the papers were finalized, we were able to bring Melissa home. Rocky and I decided when we first adopted that we weren't going to let our children know that they were adopted because we wanted our children to have a sense of family and belonging. In particular, I wanted them to know that they belonged with the rest of the children in our family and not be treated differently or as outsiders.

Though it is not an excuse for my actions, I do want to share that it was not with malicious intent that we made these decisions, but the way of thinking to which my family was accustomed. We were raised in a very traditional way, in small towns that did not recognize the nuances of race and ethnicity.

Throughout the process, although the agency told us that paperwork and other legalities would take some time, there was no formal training or paperwork about transracial adoption.

After the adoption, our adoption attorney mentioned yearly barbeques to meet up with other adoptive families that were also fundraisers to help other children in the orphanages. After we arrived home from Colombia two years later with Melissa's (adoptive) brother, there still were no check-ins from the agency other than when they sent us their congratulations.

As Melissa grew up, there were many questions. There were many times when she asked me why she was born in Colombia. I dodged that bullet by simply saying that we were there at the right time. Truth be told, at that point in time, I was afraid to tell her the truth.

Eventually, Melissa started college and met a very handsome young man who was half Colombian himself—he is now her husband. On a trip home from a break in college, Melissa was still very curious about her origins and decided to go looking around for answers and found a copy of some of her adoption paperwork in a desk drawer. She then gave it to her boyfriend and he confirmed that they were adoption papers. Melissa decided to confront me with the truth and I could no longer keep the lie. I told her my reasons, and that I loved her. We went through very turbulent times following that night. She moved out for almost a year, with barely an occasional hello. Her heart was broken, but so was mine. In my mind, I never thought of my children as being adopted.

After a year of conversation and figuring out how to be mother and daughter again, Melissa and I began to really talk. We had many conversations where she taught me that speaking out loud about adoption was okay and, among other things, it made me love her more.

Today, Melissa is an author, a mother, and a wife. She has two children and they are my world. She wrote *What White Parents Should Know about Transracial Adoption* to give tools to parents who, like me, weren't prepared to raise children of color. Fortunately, Melissa and I overcame our torrential waters, but that is not the case for everyone.

This book has helped teach me that there are still people being treated differently for their race and ethnicity. I've also learned that even though I really believed that I was not a racist person, that I had prejudices and biases that were unintentional. I've learned of so many instances where people of color are being treated horribly that I was unaware of because I was sheltered growing up.

Melissa has done a lot of research to prepare parents of today to avoid making the same mistakes that were made years ago by inexperienced people like my husband and myself. Her book gives prospective adoptive parents the information they need so that they can see what is coming before they make the decision to adopt. It gives the knowledge, the information, the tools, and everything else needed to start on the right path.

There are a lot of children who suffer from adoptive parents not dealing with today's hurtful reality. It is difficult, to say the least, when a child comes home from school and tells you that they are being made fun of for the color of their skin or how they speak, and you don't know how to make them feel better about themselves. This book helps prepare parents through all of that. It doesn't hold back, but speaks the absolute truth. It taught me a lot that I did not know before, and because of it, I have a better relationship with my children. Even though reading this may be difficult for some, as an adoptive parent myself, I have realized that taking the time to work through my feelings and learn about race is essential to being a parent of a child of color.

I may still be learning, but knowledge is power. And I recommend anyone who has adopted, or is thinking about adoption, take the time to work through this book—it is the right step in doing right by your children.

PAULA GUIDA,
*Author's mother*

# PREFACE:
## QUESTIONS ADOPTIVE PARENTS MAY HAVE WHILE READING THIS BOOK

When the idea of a book on adoption popped into my head, I knew the road to writing it would be difficult. Most materials about adoption are written by adoptive parents, mental health professionals, or adoption agencies. Few books are written from the perspective of an adoptee, especially a transracial adoptee. This book was born from the crevices of my soul that felt that if adoptive parents like my own had a resource that discussed the actual nuances and complexities of adoption, it might ease the struggles of transracial adoptees like me.

Adoptees are often the most underrepresented group in the adoption community. Despite being the ones with actual lived experience on the effects of adoption, our input is commonly undervalued and even criticized. I've created a platform based on elevating adoptee voices, for as a transracial adoptee, I believe with my whole heart that we are the best experts on adoption. My Instagram, podcast, and website, *Adoptee Thoughts*, center around the premise that adoptee voices should be prioritized and that the adoption community can make valuable changes based on our input. In turn I created this text not as an act of hate or anger, but as an olive branch to prospective and current adoptive parents.

Before we begin, I'd like to address the elephant in the room. I've learned that my writing can be challenging to read and that many adoptive parents and prospective adoptive parents can get frustrated or even defensive after reading my takes on adoption; that my thoughts on the adoption industry and problems that need to be addressed can make it sound as if I'm just an angry adoptee against adoption. I'm often asked why I'm pointing out the problems, why I'm focusing on the negative, and most importantly, what adoptive parents *should* do, and in turn, why I'm not pointing out the solution to the problems.

The answer is simple: adoptive parents hold power in a flawed system that often prioritizes adoptive parents' desires over the adopted child's and birth family's needs. My goal is to advocate for adoptees' voices that are often pushed to the side in favor of the dominant narrative from the adoptive parents' perspectives. It is important to remember that when adoptive parents hold such power in our community, they are the ones who drive the supply and demand in the adoption industry and, therefore, impact the laws and regulations that are passed. The way adoptive parents choose to invest their money can help promote changes in the industry and pressure agencies to do better.

According to the *social exchange theory*, humans form and maintain relationships when they believe the benefits or rewards will be greater than the costs. Adoptive parents typically have status, information, money, and so on that they may use to enter into a relationship with those who have children available for adoption (i.e., adoption agencies).[1] The power that adoptive parents hold stems from the weight of the money they bring into the adoption industry and how the industry caters to their desires and needs. Yes, birth parents can have *some* power, but the power swings to adoptive parents once the adoption papers are finalized. Afterward, adoptive parents can choose what information to share with their children, how much access birth parents have to children in open adoptions, and whether or not they do further research about adoption trauma, nurturing cultural identity, and more.

Let's think about the adoption industry as an old house that has been in our family for ages—it has provided shelter for many families, it can keep out the rain and animals, and it can keep us warm. However, without upkeep and improvements over the years, the house loses its value and becomes unsafe to live in. Similarly, without modifications to the adoption industry, its practices can become problematic and unethical if oversight is not upheld and parents aren't properly educated. This is why we must listen to adult adoptees and invest back into programs and agencies that learn from new studies emphasizing the importance of cultural immersion and educating parents in that area.

Right now, the speed of adoption tends to be the number one consideration that adoptive parents look at with agencies. Still, promoting and investing in agencies that prioritize pre- and post-educational support for transracial adoptions can encourage agencies to put more effort into these crucial programs. The truth is, millions of couples are looking to adopt in America. Suppose the adoption system could screen prospective adoptive parents properly for biases and begin training programs for potential parents. In that case, it could immediately rule out prospective adoptive parents who are not ready or who are unwilling to do the work.

I frequently find that adoptive parents often promote fundraisers to raise the cost of home studies and lawyer fees. I never see adoptive parents raising money for education and workshops for transracial education. Many adoptive parents acknowledge that they did not realize the importance of educational programs and support for transracial adoption until after they adopted. Rachel Garlinghouse (an adoptive parent) wrote a personal essay for Scary Mommy explaining how adopting her Black son was a wake-up call for their adoptive family. It was only after seeing how people went from seeing her son as handsome when he was a baby and little boy to seeing him as a criminal when he grew taller and bigger that she realized the depth of systemic racism in American society.[2] The purpose of this book is to bring awareness to couples before they adopt, so their wake-up call isn't after their child has dealt with the consequences of a "love is enough" mentality, and to explain why white saviorism and promotion of toxic positivity is a problem.

Before we begin, I want to address some of the most pressing questions that adoptive parents have asked other adoptees and me. Some of these questions and their answers may seem offensive and problematic. However, I genuinely believe that the only way that we can grow is by having honest conversations without shying away from more challenging topics.

*NOTE* *If you are an adoptee, you may want to skip this section because some questions can be triggers.*

**Why focus on the negative?**    There is no one-size-fits-all way to view adoption. It is multifaceted and complicated. Elevating only the positive angle of adoption is a disservice to every part of the triad. (The adoption triad refers to the three groups in the adoption community: adoptive parents, birth parents, and adoptees.) To have adoptive parents go into adoption with a savior mentality is detrimental, not only for the adoptee, but for the adoptive parents and birth parents. It creates an imbalance of power so that an adoptee "owes" their adoptive parents for "saving" them. Perpetuating the savior mentality emphasizes that something is inherently negative about their birth parents—that they are less than.

As humans, it is our natural inclination to make comparisons between people and things in our lives. As toddlers, we learn that from simple activities: we choose the bigger dinosaur over the smaller one, the pile of candy that has more chocolate. It's normal to make comparisons between parents; we notice one parent is stronger and can give piggyback rides or that the other is better at drawing cartoons and making funny voices. When you enter a family dynamic with adoption, you have more parents in the equation than a traditional family does, and this can lead to even more comparisons.

And yes, that means your transracial children recognize that their skin color is different than yours and similar to their birth parents'.

Studies show that children can identify race between the ages of four and six, and other races become aware of racial/ethnic groups at around seven years old. However, from as young as five, children of color show a preference for whiteness and downplay their identities as people of color; this can be seen through their preference for white dolls or pictures of white individuals. It has also been found that white children in preschool can start using racist language and discriminating against integrating their playgroups to include Black children.[3] Other studies show that infants as young as three months can indicate a preference for faces from particular racial groups, and nine-month-old babies can use race to categorize different faces. By age four, children in the United States have been found to associate white people with higher wealth and status.[4]

Children notice if there are no other people of color around your family.

They notice when you pick apart or criticize their birth parents.

And they notice when relatives, friends, and strangers thank you for being so selfless and say things like how "they could never adopt."

And despite how happy adopted children appear to be, or even say they are, they will appear to be "unhappy" or "ungrateful" adopted children at some point in their lives if they offer criticism about adoption.

This is why we need to discuss the negative.

Your child will need help processing these negative emotions and self-destructive thoughts, as well as negative cognitions and insecurities, with you or a professional therapist, mentor, or others. Your child will need someone who understands racism, cultural differences, bullies, and feeling isolated. And as their adoptive parent, you must have the skills to help them healthily process these negative emotions rather than deny them or shut them down.

And the main reason I advocate so frequently for discussing the negative aspects of adoption is that adoptees are four times more likely to attempt suicide.[5] *Four times.* Let that sink in for a second.

In addition to higher suicide attempts, adoptees are also at an increased risk of having depression, anxiety, ADHD or ADD, oppositional defiant disorder, and other mental illnesses. And, according to research, adoptees are also about five times more likely to be addicted to drugs and about two to three times more likely to commit crimes than other children.[6]

There are reasons for that. And I firmly believe we need to bring more concrete research and attention to these issues to help adoptees as they grow up in adoptive homes and face challenges non-adopted children do not experience.

**Isn't adopting better than being stuck in an orphanage?**  Why is this a question important for you to reflect on when someone is pointing out flaws in a system you benefited from?

Being stuck in an orphanage for the rest of your life is arguably not a good option, but is deeply problematic when the response to people sharing systemic issues and personal experiences with trauma is stating that "it could be worse." The truth is that many people could have had worse upbringings. Many people could've had worse parents. And many parents, including white adoptive parents, have always tried their best. But just because you tried your best or you did not know you were hurting your child does not excuse you from acknowledging the harm and trauma many transracial adoptees have experienced.

It is always easier to focus on the positives portrayed in the media that focus on adoptive parents saving children of color from an eternal life of suffering in orphanages. When the news, social media, and movies portray the cookie-cutter version of a perfect adoption story, where a beautiful white couple adopts a Black, Brown, Indigenous, or Asian orphan, it ties up a flawed system in a pretty bow that is easier for the masses to accept. It allows us to see adoption as the happily-ever-after answer. Viewing adoption as infallible is more comfortable than admitting and magnifying the adoption industry's enormous flaws—the lack of education, training, and support pre- and post-adoption.

Adoption is complicated. Adoption is nuanced. Adoption is trauma. And just because it's beautiful sometimes, does not mean that we shouldn't strive to make it better or that we should fail to acknowledge its flaws. Dismissive questions like this one deflect from the systemic issues at large in favor of recognizing adoptive parents for "saving" children. As if the questions should excuse adoptive parents from being held to account for problematic parenting that can cause further trauma to an already vulnerable population.

Just because adoptees are coming from an orphanage or the foster care system does not make it okay for adoptive parents to accept subpar efforts from adoption agencies, nor does it give them an excuse not to do the work. Millions of couples are looking to adopt, but not all are willing to do more than the bare minimum. A couple willing to do anti-racism work and consistently incorporate their adopted child's culture into their day-to-day is a better candidate than a couple who isn't. Adoption agencies should show a preference for choosing adoptive parents who are willing to do this work rather than focusing on the amount of money they can bring in from a child's adoption. Adoption is a business in which more couples are seeking to adopt than there are babies available for adoption. If we raise our standards instead of focusing on the money and speed of adoptions, we can help make ethical changes that will affect the lives of transracial adoptive families for the better.

**Is adoption bad?**   The age-old question: Is adoption bad? Or, put another way, Am I a bad person for adopting or wanting to adopt? There is no simple answer to this. Some wholeheartedly believe that adoption is evil; some enthusiastically believe it is not only good but almost an act of God. But we'll get into more of that later.

My point here is to help you see that the answer isn't simple. To say adoption is entirely one or the other does a disservice to all of those in the adoption triad and can, frankly, be very disrespectful. If you have adopted or are planning to adopt, your role as a parent needs to elevate respecting your adoptee's and other adoptees' beliefs and experiences. When you come across an adoptee who challenges how you view adoption, sit with that uncomfortable feeling and reflect.

As you read this book, at many points you may feel frustrated, angry even, sad, defensive, or just uncomfortable. And that, my friend, is a good thing. In order to grow and learn enough information about transracial adoption to be a *good* adoptive parent, you need to expand beyond your own comfortable world view and bubble. Listen to voices that challenge your beliefs, and take this time to grow as a person.

One of the hardest and yet arguably the most important parts of being a parent, I've found, is accepting that I will make mistakes and giving myself and my children the due we deserve by striving to learn and do better.

**Aren't you afraid you'll scare people from adopting?** To be completely transparent, this is more often an accusation than an honest question. My answer is no. That there are those who are "scared" so easily from adopting because I, other adoptees, birth moms, or even some adoptive parents discuss the complications and darker sides of adoption does not make me worried that it will suddenly deter all adoptive parents and leave millions of innocent kids stranded in orphanages.

Adoption has gone through various stages of popularity within countries, but in the United States, in particular, there has and always will be a desire to have young babies available for adoption. Particularly white babies.

**Why aren't Black, Indigenous, or other persons of color adopting?** People of color are interested in adopting but can face discrimination when trying to get approved for fostering or adoption. Only about 1 percent of potential Black adoptive parents are approved whereas about 10 percent of white applicants are.[7] We will discuss this more in Chapter 3.

**I know someone who was adopted and they have no complaints; doesn't their opinion matter?** Just because you know happy adoptees doesn't magically make adoption perfect for everyone. And it most definitely doesn't negate the adoptee's or birth parent's valid feelings about adoption. If you find yourself accusing an adoptee who is talking about adoption negatively of being an "angry adoptee" or an "ungrateful adoptee," you need to take a step back and reevaluate why you are trying to make them feel bad about their feelings and experiences.

Ask yourself these questions:

- Why might this adoptee feel this way?

- Why does their opinion make me so uncomfortable and defensive?

- How would I feel if I opened up about something that hurt me and people dismissed my feelings simply because they knew someone who was happy who had experienced something similar?

**Why do my kids never mention these supposed problems?** We were in the midst of #BlackLivesMatter protests and efforts to end systemic racism within police departments and throughout America in 2020 when I once again mentioned the protests in passing to my parents. Before I could complete the phrase "Black Lives . . ." my mother enthusiastically interjected, "All lives matter!"

Now, I could have ignored her, changed the subject, or just hung up the phone, but my blood was boiling after days of watching videos of Black protesters being brutalized by police, children being gassed, and an old white man bleeding after he was pushed to the ground by police who walked past him as if nothing had happened . . . all because these people were fighting for equity. So instead of hiding behind my privilege as a mixed-race Latina and the protection of being in proximity to my white family all of my life, I corrected her.

"No, Mom, Black people are being murdered time and time again by police. The system is unjust, and people of color, especially Black people, are being targeted. Their lives have been taken while in their homes, on the street, and when they should have been treated with human dignity. It's not okay. And saying 'all lives matter' is problematic, and I refuse to allow you to say that to me."[8]

I was passionate, yet firm, and still, my pleas for her to understand went on deaf ears. It is beyond difficult to have deep discussions about race and your own personal experiences with racism and then have them ignored, denied, or even mocked. This is why I often avoided these types of conversations with my parents before my father passed away; it is easier to push this problem aside in order to maintain the stability that we have in our relationship. If I were to be completely honest and bring up all the issues I've had with racism and even microaggressions within my own family, I would be afraid to hurt my parents' feelings when I know they were just doing their best.

This is just one reason why adopted children may not speak honestly with their parents about some of the issues they have faced as transracial adoptees, but here is an expanded list that may open your eyes to some of the challenges adoptees face.

**Why Some Adopted Children Keep Quiet about Problems They've Experienced as Adoptees**

1. **Guilt.** We don't want to make our adoptive parents feel bad and don't want to be seen as ungrateful.

2. **Fear.** We are afraid of rejection, denial, anger, and abandonment. It can be terrifying to open up to our white adoptive parents about racism. We do not want our parents to have any excuse to abandon us when we often already feel like our first families have.

3. **Shame.** We feel shame when we're told we are ungrateful for having negative feelings toward our adoption and that we are selfish for going against the grain of positive adoption language.

4. **Denial.** Society often favors a positive narrative of adoption. At times, denying the pain and trauma of being an adoptee can often be easier; we can avoid processing our complicated emotions and experiences.

5. **Need Time.** It can simply take time for us to process and come to terms with our identity problems and experiences as a transracial adoptee. And we may not be comfortable sharing that part of our journey with our parents until we are ready.

6. **Need to Belong.** Being adopted already subjects us to experiences that other people do not have to go through, but speaking about these to our adoptive parents can make this seem more real. It can even be ostracizing to further admit we are more different and point out the issues that we may face from being an adoptee.

# INTRODUCTION

"I want to adopt a child someday to give them a better life."

This is a sentiment that is often said by prospective parents to their peers, friends, and anyone who will listen.

This narrative is influenced by viral videos we see online, advertisements of impoverished neighborhoods in third-world countries on TV, and discussions in some churches that urge attendees to give the *gift* of adoption.

But what exactly is adoption? When you look up the definition on the web, it says adoption typically takes place when a nonbiological parent becomes the legal parent to a child. But somehow this somewhat neutral definition has been erased in favor of an overarching positive theme that warms the hearts of others. Often adoption is recast to represent a family, often a white couple, who is "saving" a child in need.

In fact, over 70 percent of adoptive parents in the United States are white and 84 percent of transracially adoptive parents in the United States are white, making transracial adoptions more and more visible in today's world.[1,2] At a glance, this may seem like a promising statistic because it means adoptive families are becoming more inclusive racially. After all, from the outside looking in, cute Instagram photos of white families with their happy Brown or Black babies holding felt letterboards can seem like the perfect solution to providing babies with homes and increasing multiculturalism in the US.

There's just a little problem.

The ideas that love is enough and color doesn't matter are also prevalent. These ideas can cause adoptees to grow up in homes in which their parents ignore their race and society tells them to be happy with what they've got. These views perpetuate the idea that adoptees need to be grateful no matter their circumstances; if they aren't, they are instantly viewed as the ungrateful adoptee.

An *ungrateful adoptee* criticizes the adoption system and their adoptive parents and often portrays a more complex view of adoption than the public often accepts. When we speak out against adoption issues, we are almost automatically given the title of ungrateful because many people see our speech as a threat to finding homes for other children in need. However, our intention is not that—instead, we are focused on improving a flawed system that has harmed adoptees, birth moms, and even adoptive parents.

You may be wondering what this means. If there are problems within the system, does that mean that adoption is bad? Does it mean that adoption shouldn't happen?

Adult adoptees, specifically those who have been adopted transracially, have started to advocate for the rights of adopted children and to bring to light the challenges in the system, even though the nuances are often difficult to discuss in quick exchanges on Twitter threads or by answering Facebook group questions. Despite the challenges, adult adoptees continuously try to relay their experiences publicly online with essays, threads, memoirs, and videos about their trauma. To help shape a more honest narrative, they openly discuss racial identity, finding birth families, and even racism in their own homes. However, adoptive parents and other members of society do not frequently meet these real-life stories with compassion or show interest in further discussion. These adoptees are often shut down with gaslighting, aggression, and, sometimes, threats. These are some examples of common responses adoptees receive:

*Would you rather have been aborted?*

*You don't know what you're talking about; my friend was adopted, and she's happy.*

*Would you rather have been left in an orphanage?*

*You should be grateful for the life you have!*

*Go back to where you were born if you're so unhappy.*

*Think about your parents! How would they feel hearing you speak like that?!*

I could go on and on. The insults and accusations that I have heard since talking about my adoption story so publicly have hit home more than once. It is hard to hear people become so angry with me, but I'm now used to it. From the moment I found out I was adopted and tried to discuss the complicated range of emotions caused by my adoption experience, my feelings have often been dismissed by parents, friends, and even some other adoptees.

*Would you rather we left you there? What do you think your life would have been like?*

As adoption stories go, mine is a tad bit more complicated than most because I am not just a *transracial* (adopted by parents of a different race) and *international adoptee* (adopted from a different country), but I am also a *late-discovery adoptee*. This means that I wasn't told that I was adopted as a child; instead, I discovered that I was adopted when I was an adult. I was nineteen years old, and it completely changed my life. I faced identity problems and felt completely isolated.

Due to my adoptive family's multicultural roots, they were able to claim that my darker skin came from distant relatives. Even though I had many questions about my identity during my adolescence, I was met with simple answers and no-nonsense attitudes that left me feeling that I had little room to argue. Once my adoption came to light, I had even more questions as I struggled to figure out the new pieces of my identity, especially since I grew up in a family that had deep prejudices against people who were of a different race/ethnicity.

After a few conversations with my (adoptive) parents about the issues that I was experiencing as an adoptee, and after even more conversations with new adoptee friends I met on Facebook groups online, I realized that my experience was not that different from my adoptee peers. A lot of us have struggled with our identities and with our mental health, and many of us have even experienced racism within our adoptive families. After seeing this correlation time and time again within the adoptee community, I realized that the adoption narrative the world has focused on was not the same as what I and other transracial adoptees have experienced.

I tried discussing these issues with my parents and was met with argumentative comments and questions about why I was so angry and ungrateful. It wasn't that I didn't love my parents or have a decent childhood; it was the fact that their frequent response of "it could have been worse" seemed like their excuse for not dealing with the issues I *did* face, which leads me to the reason why I am writing this book—to help educate adoptive parents about a more nuanced approach to transracial adoption that elevates the voices of adoptees who, in my opinion, are the experts because we have the lived experience.

You may be thinking that stories like mine are few and far between—that this doesn't really happen all that much. But that is not the case. I've found that many adoptees have similar stories to mine and have also struggled with their identities and how they fit in.

The attacks I have seen hurled at fellow adoptees who are simply telling the most heart-wrenching stories about their childhood and experiences just keep coming. This experience is all too common, and not just with late-discovery adoptees like myself; it is also especially prevalent within transracial adoptions in general. Because of this backlash, all comments by adoptees and adoptive parents that I've included in this book were taken from confidential interviews. The names of interviewees have been withheld by mutual agreement.

If you've done any research into adoption, you have probably found that most books, guides, movies, and even news stories are told from the adoptive parent's perspective. The voices of adoptees, who have experienced beauties as well as struggles from adoption, are often underappreciated. But adoptees have a lot of insight and help to offer adoptive parents that will not only help the adopted child but will also help the whole community grow and prosper.

My mission is to create an open dialogue in which adoptee voices can be prioritized so that the adoption community can come together to create beneficial change for us all. Adoptive parents are too often portrayed as the heroes in the story who set out to give a child a better life (or, at least, what most people think of as a better life according to modern society's standards). The idea that the system is imperfect is one that goes against the very core belief that many adoptive parents hold dear.

One of the greatest fears of an adoptive parent is their child being hurt by something that they were told was beautiful and amazing by everyone they know. How can there be flaws in the very thing that brought them what they desired most—a child? How can loving a baby be bad? How can saving a baby be bad?

When I first started to talk to my (adoptive) mother about my thoughts on adoption, she grew very angry and defensive. Yes, as an adult, I could have probably broached topics more sensitively, but initially, I was carrying a lot of pain and resentment associated with our relationship. After all, she hid my adoption for so many years. When I talked to her about certain issues that show up in transracial and international adoption practices, she often shut down or hurt me with her reaction.

One time she said to me, "I get it. You hate adoption. I should never have done what I did. I get it. I'm evil."

Her words dripped with sarcasm, anger, resentment, and pain. And this is what made me realize that we needed a way to discuss the topics that are important to transracial adoptees. Comments like these can threaten the idea that adoptive parents can be "real parents" and "good parents" if their children's lives aren't perfect. The reality is that no parent is perfect, we all make mistakes. With this book, I hope to find a way to cross that bridge that is often rife with many emotions from all sides of the triad to help us all come together and to do what is best for transracially adopted children and adults. If we all can push aside pride, anger, and resentment, and respect one another's truths, if we can learn and grow from actual research and lived experiences of adoptees, we can help improve lives. We can make a difference. But the only way we can do this is by coming together. By sitting with topics that can make us uncomfortable, that make us defensive, sad, and sometimes angry. To do this, we need to acknowledge why this mentality is a problem and why it happens, and then we need to explore different, realistic solutions to do away with it that are helpful for all involved in the triad.

This book is a tool for those who are willing to learn more and become allies to make changes to the complicated system of adoption. We will explore adoption and white privilege, the history of adoption, and how, as an industry, it can harm adoptees, trigger adoptive parents, and cause identity issues. The book also includes interviews with adoptive parents and adult adoptees to provide a complete picture of the experience. As a whole, this material focuses on the challenges transracial adoptees face, but it branches out a bit to explore the effects of toxic positivity in the adoption community as a whole.

Although the title of this book implies that the audience is only white adoptive parents, this text should speak to all parts of the triad. At times, adoptive parents reading this material may become defensive. But as I explained earlier, this is all a natural process of coming out of the fog. I urge you to take your time, begin discussions with adult adoptees or a therapist, or even write in a journal for a time before you react to the information this text provides. If you are an adoptee, this book can help you understand the experiences you may have gone through. If you are a birth parent, it might influence your decision when placing your child.

Adoption is a multifaceted experience for everyone involved, but we can learn from one another to help prevent trauma if we just open our hearts to the fact that all of our experiences and feelings are valid.

I include interviews with adoptees as well as parents who have adopted transracially to help open a conversation from which others can learn. I cover raw and honest takes on the nuances of adoption in this book, so please take a second to reflect before you dive in. To make change and progress, we need to listen, learn, and work together.

# 1

# THE CHALLENGES OF
# TALKING TO WHITE ADOPTIVE
# PARENTS ABOUT RACE

When I asked my mom why she lied about me being adopted, she said that she was afraid that I would be treated differently and that she was worried our extended family wouldn't love me the way they did the other kids in the family. I didn't have to ask why, specifically, because I knew. I knew growing up that my white, middle-class family had strong prejudices. I had heard the stereotypes and bigoted statements often enough from my parents, aunts, uncles, and cousins.

What I wished my mother knew back in the nineties was that she would never be able to protect me from feeling different. No matter how often my family denied my ancestry and taught me to pretend that I was white, society would never accept that.

*Why do people think I can speak Spanish? Why do they look at me as if I'm stupid and then act surprised when I speak perfect English?*

I asked my parents such questions over and over. I spent a lot of my time hurt, angry, and frustrated because I didn't have answers, and the racism and microaggressions nagged at me year after year despite my parents' assurances that their reactions didn't matter.

*Why does everyone think I am Hispanic?*

Because I was.

The way my parents raised me reflected their cultures. But from a very young age, despite not knowing the truth about my adoption, I was constantly pulled toward the music and people of my Colombian roots. Most of my close friends were other people of color—I just fit in better with the people who looked like me. They understood what it was like to have people judge you based on skin tone, to have racist relatives, and to stand out in our mostly white, middle-class suburban community.

And yet, when I questioned my parents about my ethnicity and race, I was always told I was not one of *them*. It didn't matter what others thought or how I was treated—because I was Italian in their eyes. Because if I was Colombian, I didn't belong. From their perspective, my adoption was supposed to give me a better life, and if they admitted that I faced racial problems, that I was viewed as a Latina, that meant they couldn't protect me and save me like they thought they had. I was living a good life, a great life even, where color *didn't* matter to my parents. We had a white picket fence, lived in a perfect suburban neighborhood, had food on the table every night. Heck, sometimes there was too much food.

*What did I have to complain about?*

But even in the picture-perfect environment my parents provided, they couldn't protect me from racism. Especially their own. To admit that they couldn't protect me was unthinkable because it went against the white savior mentality that they held dear. How could I be unhappy when they had saved me from an impoverished country? From an orphanage in Colombia? From a place where no one wanted me but them?

Despite their love, despite the material possessions that they provided—necessities that they were able to afford—they could not get past their colorblindness like so many other white adoptive parents. To admit that I was treated differently was to admit that they weren't perfect. They couldn't protect me . . . even from themselves. My storybook happily-ever-after ending as an adoptee was a lie, and that was too hard for them to swallow.

When I first started engaging in conversations with my parents about my transracial adoption, I was met with immediate resistance. Their reluctance was as formidable as the thick wall they had put up to hide my adoption from me for nineteen years. At first, I thought my experience with my (adoptive) parents was unique—that they were different than other white adoptive parents.

I was wrong.

I had thought I was the problem for years. But after I entered more online adoption communities for adoptees, even some that included adoptive parents, it became obvious that this was not the case.

The experiences that fellow transracial adoptees openly discussed seemed to be primarily negative to my eyes. Almost every post I clicked contained horrible experiences of racism, colorblindness, and, sometimes, blatant abuse from adoptive parents. The stories I heard were all over the spectrum. Still, the overarching theme was that adoptive parents did not respect the culture of their adopted children whom they loved; they espoused anything from common microaggressions to overt racism.

*My parents refused to talk about race.*

*My aunt always called me an Asian princess, and my mom said I had to let her.*

*My dad talked about the construction workers and complained about them talking in Spanish. He always said it meant they were up to something. I'm Latino, and he wouldn't let me learn to speak Spanish.*

*Yeah, well, my parents were abusive, and I dealt with physical and even sexual abuse.*

These comments are examples of real, first-person reports I have witnessed in adoption communities; to say I was shocked and in disbelief at first was an understatement.

The idea that adoption could be a bad thing had never crossed my mind before I joined these groups. To me, finding out adoptees were hurting was almost as unbelievable as me finding out at nineteen that I was adopted. To relate to their experiences meant, in my mind, that I never had a chance to be happy. Anger took over quickly, and because I was so overwhelmed, I found myself leaving each group to protect the positive narrative of adoption I had known up to that point. That narrative made me feel better and it allowed me to avoid facing emotions I had never had to address before.

All of my life, I had been inundated with the same media influences as my white adoptive parents. I believed that adopting was saving a child. I believed that children in impoverished neighborhoods were lucky when celebrities and upper-middle-class white parents adopted them. The videos on the news and the stories in the paper of Black and Brown babies being picked up from the airport made me happy. But now I had to digest that this system that I thought was beautiful wasn't as perfect as I thought.

My world flipped upside down. I was experiencing my adoption in a new light, or as the adoption community calls it, I was coming *out of the fog.*

According to research by Judith Penny on reconstructing adoption issues, adoptees go through five phases: not being aware of adoption issues, becoming aware, drowning in these issues, reemerging from awareness, and finding a sense of peace.[1] This study helped the adoption community realize that adoption-reconstruction phases were nonlinear. *Adoption reconstruction* refers to the ongoing process of reconstructing the concept and meaning of adoption and was chosen specifically to reflect the ongoing complex and dynamic process.[2] What this meant was that it was normal for me to feel angry, sad, and then fine in no particular order. It was normal for me to go for days and weeks with anger storming through my bloodstream like an infection and then at other times, I'd have a day that was like a tornado of all of the feelings at once.

Coming out of the fog was like making it through the craziest storm I had ever seen. I yearned for the calm after, where everything would make sense and I would no longer be in pain. But when I tried to open up to my family about the loss and trauma in adoption . . . well, they denied my experiences so wholeheartedly that I almost thought I was in the wrong—that I was crazy.

The narrative that I was told by everyone was that my parents had saved me from a horrible life, and that being unhappy as an adoptee meant that I hated my parents. I felt incredibly guilty for making my parents feel unloved or unneeded, even for a moment, and so I decided that it was best if I drop the subject. After all, I had a good life, a better life than most, and I believed that I should be grateful to be given more than what I believed many orphans could hope to one day obtain.

Years passed before I could work up the courage to talk about my adoption story again. I went back and forth through the five phases, thinking about the life that I could have had, thinking about a culture that I knew nothing about, and then cycling back to thinking that my adoption hadn't mattered in the grand scheme of life.

It was only after I started going to therapy that I learned that adoption, like many things in life, is nuanced. By viewing the impacts of adoption as black and white, I was doing the entire adoption industry and community a disservice. I learned that it is in the shades of gray that we can find the beauty of some things as well as the parts that need work.

The very positive narrative we are fed can often make us (adoptees) feel very conflicted when we have more complex feelings than we expect, and because of this, I immediately felt the need to try and make things better for adoptees. Once I saw the impacts of adoption as gray, I finally could face the reality that my trauma was real, and that adoption wasn't a perfect solution without flaws. Accepting this empowered me to want to open up—not only to adoptees and adoptive parents but to potential adoptive parents—by making my voice heard online and in the media.

After all, I thought, how can we make changes to a system unless we talk more about its flaws?

## ADOPTION AND WHITE PRIVILEGE

There's this idea (that even fellow adoptees have) that adopting a child of color and providing a loving and nurturing home makes adoptive parents immune to being racist. Maybe in an ideal world that would be true, but unfortunately, this is not an ideal world. Adopting a child of color does not mean that you aren't racist, just like having a best friend who is a BIPOC (Black, Indigenous, or person of color) doesn't mean you're not racist.

Recently I was reminded of this idea by a fellow international adoptee who messaged me privately in September of 2020; he said that he "never realized how much hate there is from adopted children of color who have white parents." He went on to deny that my parents, and other white adoptive parents could possibly be racist toward their adoptive children of color. This, admittedly, hurt since it came from another adoptee who was basically dismissing my lived experiences of racism within my own family, along with those of many other adoptees. This message was a vivid reminder that not all adoptees have the same experience. Because the positive narrative of adoption is so prevalent, another adoptee found it difficult to believe my adoptive parents could be racist, despite having heard and read about several accounts from adoptees who experienced racism within their families.

The article posted on Medium by Melea VanOstrand, titled "'I'm Not Racist. I Have a Black Family Member!' I'm That Black Family Member, and Yes, You Are Racist," includes many gems, but one line stood out to me as a transracial adoptee in a white family.[3] It described the response Melea had to her sister saying that she didn't see her as Black, that she was simply her sister. VanOstrand said, "And she's right. That's who I am to her. Not her Black sister. But, to the rest of the world, I am a Black woman. They aren't color-blind like she is."[4]

Those words hit me deep in the gut. VanOstrand eloquently stated in a few lines what I had been trying to get my family to understand for years. That despite my being "one of them," as my mom so often says, others don't view me or treat me as white, and in turn, I am not protected by their whiteness as an adult. The world views me as a Latina woman and treats me like one. They make assumptions about me that many people make about other Latina women: they assume that I speak broken English, clean homes for a living, or am otherwise "less than." They never guess that I am a college graduate who runs my own business, publishes essays in prominent magazines, and hosts my own podcast.

On the one hand, hearing my parents or family members claim me as one of them makes me feel happy that they love and care for me, but on the other hand, it makes me feel like their love is conditional and based on my assimilation into *their* culture and traditions. It's almost an unspoken rule that I do not bring up my heritage or remind them that I am different.

Despite a "love is love" or "love is enough" dominant narrative in adoption, many adopted children of color struggle with their identities, and white parents who cling to this narrative are doing their children a disservice. Love will be enough for many families until it's not, and what is important for adoptive parents to realize is that their privilege will not protect their children of color indefinitely. A time comes when all children of color face discrimination and racism, whether by strangers, friends, or family. This is why white adoptive parents need to be willing to do the work and learn how to prepare children for a world that does see color. Acknowledging the privilege of being a white adoptive parent will help you bridge the gap within your adoptive family and embrace being a multicultural family.

## HOW WHITE SAVIORS ARE BORN

In 2012, Teju Cole, a Nigerian-American novelist, coined the term *white savior industrial complex (WSIC)* in a seven-part Twitter thread response to a video titled "Kony 2012" that was blowing up on YouTube.[5] In his tweets, he said that white saviorism is not about justice but about having a big emotional experience that validates privilege in which white saviors "support brutal policies in the morning, fund charities in the afternoon, and receive awards in the evening."[6] When we look at transracial adoption and consider how it was created, it is hard to ignore the systemic racism that has supported it.

Studies have shown that Black families are more likely to be investigated, reported, and have their children placed in out-of-home care than white children. Families of color were also more likely to be reported for neglect and/or abuse despite data that has shown no difference between races in rates of child abuse. In 2009 in Wisconsin, African Americans made up 8 percent of the population, but 54 percent of the children in foster care, whereas white children made up around 80 percent of the population, yet only 37 percent of the children in foster care.[7]

The idea that adoptive parents, particularly white adoptive parents, have—that they are the ones who can "offer a child a better life"—is problematic at best. I have included some of the reasons why adoptive parents chose adoption from an anonymous survey I conducted of over 100 adoptive families, and a few are as follows:[8]

> We fostered to adopt. There were so many kids that needed help and then a forever home.

> Naïvely felt there was a need (China, one-child policy).

> Children needed a family, and we love children.

> She had special needs that couldn't be treated in her country, and I knew her from my years spent living in her country.

As you can see, many times, adoptive parents expressed that they felt that they had a lot to offer children in need, whether financially, emotionally, or through better schooling or access to doctors. But when we sit down and dig into statistics and research, the data does not match up with the "need" for white adoptive parents to swoop in and adopt children. In fact, the desire of (often wealthy) adoptive parents to find a child to adopt can lead to gaps in the supply that may be filled by coercion and manipulation. One example is a couple who was led to believe they were adopting an orphan from Uganda; in actuality, the child had a family.[9]

The couple had decided to open their hearts and home to another child from an impoverished country because they believed what they refer to now as propaganda, that those children were the most in need. After reading statistics that suggested that there were three million orphans in Uganda, they began their journey to adopt in 2013. They adopted a six-year-old in 2015, but it wasn't until a year and a half later that they realized the child's story and what the agency told them was not adding up. The little girl's family had been told that a wealthy American family was simply going to sponsor their child, and they had never knowingly relinquished their parental rights. This family is just one of many that have been separated through unlawful international adoption practices.[10]

Unfortunately, due to advertisements on many TV shows, television commercials, and radio interviews, people in poorer countries are often depicted as helpless and in need of others to come save them. Mission trips to third-world countries are often rife with pictures or descriptions of starving orphaned children, and this propaganda feeds into the idea that white adoptive parents need to swoop in to "save" the many orphans who have been supposedly abandoned, abused, or worse. According to a report by Save the Children, four out of five "orphans" have one or both parents alive. Often disease, poverty, disability, disasters, and discrimination are why so many children are placed in orphanages.[11] Due to these hardships, it is not uncommon for families to place children in orphanages for periods of up to a year until they can get on their feet again.

Unfortunately, governments often see placing children in institutions as the most straightforward option rather than supporting the parents in need or addressing the root causes in the society, like poverty or a lack of affordable healthcare, that pressure parents into placing their children in orphanages. And often, it is easier and more profitable for governments and agencies to support international adoption rather than provide social supports or community-based options that would provide parents with the help they need to keep and raise their children, making orphanages the last possible option.

It wasn't until 2020 that Bethany Christian Services, a global nonprofit and one of the biggest players in international adoption, announced that they were not going to renew their accreditation once it expired in March of 2021. They are now focusing their efforts on in-country services that help children find foster and adoptive families within their own country.[12] Issues like these are so often overshadowed in the media, and prospective adoptive parents are left with a cookie-cutter attitude that leaves them susceptible to buying into the white savior mentality of children *needing* to be saved through adoption.

The decline of international adoptions in the United States is often caused by tougher restrictions and laws by the adoptee's native country that are made to limit abandonment, corruption, and/or child abuse. In states like Michigan, accreditations are being made more expensive and harder to get. One such new requirement is liability insurance for anyone in a foreign country looking to adopt who would be in contact with the children.[13] Stipulations like these often make it wiser for adoption agencies to weigh how costly being shut down would be versus ending international adoption programs on their own.

It interests me, as an adoptee, that these programs feel pushed to end not after they face corruption, abuse, and other ethical issues, but when the cost becomes too high to make the programs worth continuing; their profit versus loss pressure them not to seek reaccreditation. This alone should make adoptive parents think twice about how the adoption industry functions when they prioritize profit over children's welfare. But then you add in friends, family, and strangers all feeding into the narrative by calling adoptees lucky, by telling adoptive parents that they're angels, and by telling adoptees that they should be grateful. This narrative reinforces the idea that adoptive parents are saviors, that without adoptive parents, children are destined to rot in orphanages or be raised by parents addicted to substances. The reality is far different. Yes, there are children from very unfortunate circumstances or abusive homes; however, many, many children are only in "need" of foster and adoptive placements because their parents are too poor or may be on the receiving end of a discriminatory policy, not because there is a lack of love or problems with abuse. We will delve more into how the foster care system is complex and flawed later in Chapter 3.

The savior narrative that my parents and many other adoptive or prospective adoptive parents are familiar with often emphasizes taking care of children by embracing them into the adoptive family—often without also adopting and embracing the child's birth culture, language, and first family. By focusing on saving a child in need, adoptive parents minimize the systemic racism in the adoption system that supports the overall institution of adoption. If we didn't have such a large number of white adoptive parents willing to fall for the propaganda of children needing adoption, white saviorism would not prosper. Instead, adoptive parents often cling to the story that often paints them as the heroes in adoption. And when friends and family support this narrative, adoptive parents provide little pushback to stop others from viewing them as saviors and adoptees as lucky.

A perfect example of this was the Republican outcry during the 2020 nomination of Supreme Court Justice Amy Coney Barrett, in which they earnestly said that she could not possibly be racist because she had adopted two Black children from Haiti. You can see clear examples of Barrett's white saviorism, particularly in her opening statement at the Senate Judiciary Committee Hearing, in which she made a clear distinction between her adopted children and biological children.

She said, "Vivian came to us from Haiti. When she arrived, she was so weak that we were told she might never walk or talk normally." And "John Peter joined us shortly after the devastating earthquake in Haiti, and Jesse, who brought him home, still describes the shock on JP's face when he got off the plane in wintertime Chicago."[14] The difference in her description of her adoptive children was noticeable when compared to how she described her biological children by their personality traits and hobbies. "Liam is smart, strong, and kind, and to our delight, he still loves watching movies with Mom and Dad. Ten-year-old Juliet is already pursuing her goal of becoming an author by writing multiple essays and short stories, including one she recently submitted for publication."[15]

Some may read these descriptions and feel like what I'm saying is a reach. Still, as a transracial adoptee, I am very familiar with how some adoptive parents thrive on sharing their children's adoption stories to paint themselves in a better light. Speaking from the perspective of an adoptee of color who has been attacked for not being grateful for my parents' "sacrifice," I feel that Barrett's portrayal of her adoptive children supports a white savior mentality.

When you consider how a white savior mentality applies directly in adoption, think of it as shedding light on the idea that adoptive parents are the ones directly benefiting from their so-called selfless act. When we view adoption as this holy act that is the only way to save children, we minimize the focus on systemic racism in the adoption industry—which continues to fuel the need for families to adopt children, particularly children of color—instead of raising funds to create systems to help support women and families in their time of need. If adoption was purely about helping a child in need, why would we not create more programs to support vulnerable populations and expectant women in need?

Make no mistake, Barrett knew her statement would be publicized around the world and chose her words carefully. She had a reason for her focus on her children's adoption circumstances when she could have talked about their quirky personalities, their favorite TV show, or their hobbies. But if she had, the people praising her for adopting would have lost a good opportunity to continue to praise her or claim that she couldn't be racist because she had children of color.

Baseless claims by Republicans, celebrities, and the media support adoptive parents unconditionally because of this belief that adoptive parents can do no wrong and that they cannot possibly hold any biases, especially against people of the same race as their adopted child. For many people it is instinctual to comment on Barrett's adoptive children, commending her for adopting children and highlighting their adoption as a way to prove that she embraces diversity. In fact, she has a problematic history in this area. One particular case that stands out is a 2019 dismissal of a workplace discrimination lawsuit in which she said that "the n-word is an egregious racial epithet. . . . Smith can't win by simply proving that the word was uttered. He must also demonstrate that Colbert's use of this word altered the conditions of his employment and created a hostile or abusive working environment."[16]

When people view adoption as an act to be praised, they often miss why so many adoptions occur—particularly the ones of Black and Brown babies—and how adoptive parents raise the demand for children, particularly infants.

Adoption can be a wonderful choice you can make to expand your family, but it is not simply the selfless act that many people assume it to be. The reasons couples choose adoption are multifaceted and each is deeply personal. But one of the things we should be talking about is the economic reasons birth mothers feel pushed to place their babies up for adoption. Often adoptive couples have easy access to financial and community support and yet such support is withheld from expectant moms who would prefer to keep their children.

After all, the core of white saviorism revolves around helping others in need . . . but apparently only in a self-serving manner. Isn't this what society is supporting every time it praises Barrett or other adoptive parents for their "selfless act?"

## THE FIVE STAGES OF GRIEF

Once I started to publicly discuss my story, I learned quickly that other adoptive parents and relatives typically met me with the same resistance that I'd encountered from my parents. My viral post "My Adoptive Parents Hid My Racial Identity for 19 Years," led to dozens of emails and comments from angry adoptive parents and others who felt like adoption was a miracle I should be grateful for.[17]

I received an email from an anonymous reader on April 5, 2019; in it they said:

*I just read your article in the Huffington Post and am horrified and sad. You are a human being, the only race of humans on the planet. I cannot begin to say how offensive and hurtful your words are and how racist they come across.*

Another equally angry person wrote to me on April 12, 2019.

*You have no Columbian culture—you're an American. You have American culture—or at least you should. "Your people" go by the titles of "mom" and "dad." Your rejection of them shows a colossal lack of maturity. Grow up, or do us all a favor and move back to Columbia.*

Most of the angry emails came from those who believed that I was lucky and that I didn't have the right to criticize my parents despite the trauma their actions had caused. What I found most interesting was the overwhelming responsibility others felt to protect or fight to protect my parents' reputation—parents that most had never met or even heard of before my article was published. This need for many to protect adoptive parents despite any pain they caused seemed to stem from the discord between my account and the dominant positive adoption narrative. What these people didn't know is that I had discussed sharing my story with my parents and had their support. I wonder . . . if they knew my parents supported me, would they be so angry? Would they tell me to go back to the same country they just claimed I had no ties with?

The problem with this anger is that it wasn't just aimed at me or my story. Almost every conversation, video, or blog post I read by other adoptees that discussed the difficulties adoptees face was met with anger, denial, and bargaining by adoptive parents on the internet.

In 2016, responding to an essay by Mariama J. Lockington titled "What a Black Woman Wishes Her Adoptive White Parents Knew," Madeline S. wrote the following in a public Facebook comment: " . . . she [Lockington] is a self-absorbed ingrate. Not because she was a transracial adoptee or because she was adopted at all, she had two parents who loved her and raised her, but that is not enough for her. She gloms onto the difference in skin color as an excuse to belittle the people that love her. She needs to grow up."[18]

In 2018, Steve J. made another Facebook comment to Nicole Chung's essay, "People Want to Hear That I'm Happy I Was Adopted. It's Not That Simple." He said that, "I hope no one decides against international adoption based on this lady's experience. It is atypical and probably the result of isolation in a small, remote, homogenous community."[19]

It seemed to me that any efforts to diversify the adoption narrative, especially by adoptees who were personally affected by adoption, were immediately met with aggressive efforts to shut them down. Any apparent questioning of the adoption industry brought out constant angry or even fearful responses. When I saw these types of comments repeatedly, it made me realize that many white adoptive parents seem to experience a cycle of grief when they learn about the challenges adoptive children have faced and the injustices in the adoption system. Some people refer to this as adoptive parents coming out of their own fog. More specifically, I think of this as a process that adoptive parents need to work through to become truly aware of the problems caused by the white savior mentality.

I believe that parents have to fully mourn the ideal adoption to be able to truly sympathize and empathize with their adoptees who are coming out of the fog. If they don't, the conversation and understanding between adoptive parents, birth moms, and adoptees cannot be as honest and meaningful as it needs to be to help the adoption community move in the right direction. When they learn more about the full scope of birth moms' and adoptees' adoption experiences and more of the nuanced history, adoptive parents can become overwhelmed; that is when the first stage of grief immediately kicks in.

## Denial

When many adoptive parents are first faced with the idea that their child's life has had complications, they often instinctually deny it. It is natural to get defensive about a concept that we have held near and dear to our hearts for many years. White adoptive parents in this situation are confronted with the reality that they could not protect their child from the pain of racism, isolation, and/or trauma. They also have to face the reality that they might have caused harm, which might be even more painful.

I have seen parents go so far as to delete what they deemed to be inappropriate comments on Facebook from adoptees who were sharing their life experiences or opinions, simply because it does not fit the narrative the parents wanted to project.

Personally, I have been told that I have had a wonderful life, and any problems I did share were minimized.

Ignoring another person's pain is easy as long as you keep looking in different directions, surround yourself with only people who agree with you, and simply quiet down or cancel the offender. It's easy to say "not all adoptees feel that way" when you are the person holding power in the dynamic.

As an adoptive parent, it can be hard to get open and honest feedback when adoptees and birth mothers are either afraid or too nervous to share their actual feelings. The problem is that refusing to listen or being in denial only makes the situation worse for the adoptee in the long run.

Some of the defensive comments I received from adoptive parents responding to an essay I recently published, titled "Abby Johnson's Video Shows the Problem with White Parents Adopting Children of Color," show these dynamics. This article discussed the Republican national convention speaker Abby Johnson's remarks about how it was smart for police officers to profile her Black (adopted) son but not her white sons.[20] Here is one of the comments on the post that illustrate this defensiveness:

> *Though I agree, as an adoptive parent, with much of this story, it fails to address one glaring issue. For a significant number of these children, a white adoptive home may not be the ideal placement. It is, however, the only permanent placement available to them. Whatever inadequacies the adoptive parents might have in dealing with race, "color blindness," and other issues—it is impossible to accept that these children would have been better off left to be raised in and by a broken system. Children, all children, deserve to grow up in a home where they are wanted and belong." Dena@Write-Solutions[21]*

My response to comments like these is to say that thinking that adoption is a simple either-or situation is not helpful to anyone in the adoption triad. Yes, many children need homes, but it is often because the system does not support their birth families and because flaws in the system are often ignored. After all, adoption agencies do not make their profit by helping to preserve families; they profit off of adoptions by mainly white adoptive parents.

## Anger

Once denial takes hold, adoptive parents often shift from ignoring the problem to becoming angry at people who are trying to break the perfect picture of adoption that they cherished. They may argue with their adoptive children when the adoptees discuss challenges they faced, they may lash out at adoptees and birth mothers who tell their stories in the media or online, and they may simply be aggressive toward anyone expressing an opposing viewpoint.

Anger might also crop up when adoptive parents complete the cycle of grief and swing back to the beginning stages to aim their anger toward adult adoptees, fellow adoptive parents, adoption agencies, and themselves. This can be dangerous because it can lead to a sense of hopelessness that also does not support the adoptee. Adoptive parents act this out in angry messages to transracial adoptees calling them ungrateful, publicly comment in Facebook threads arguing against adoptees' lived experiences, and even publicly shame adoption practices for unethical processes without taking responsibility for their part in them.

Once adoptive parents become aware of the ethical issues within adoption, and the lack of support for birth parents, adult adoptees, and even adoptive parents, it can be easy for some parents to become keyboard warriors toward other adoptive parents online. This shows up as snippy and even angry comments about adoption practices in adoption groups on Facebook, or as them expressing outrage about certain things, but providing little to no follow-through to support actual change.

## Bargaining

Once adoptive parents are exposed to enough conversations about the nuances of adoption, they might open up to admit problems do occur. This usually means adoptive parents are willing to accept some of the information and that they may even agree that there are more systemic issues that they do not feel individually responsible for. I've found that many adoptive parents openly admit that there are problems such as child trafficking and a lack of support for adoptees and birth parents, but they have a harder time accepting the more controversial issues.

In this stage of grief, adoptive parents openly try to discuss topics they deem acceptable but cling to phrases like "not all adoptive parents," "not all adoptees feel that way," or "but I know an adoptee who is happy even though _____ and _____ happens sometimes." They often stick to the "love is enough" narrative and ignore the problems that racism and white saviors can cause. However, once they work through these feelings, they often become distraught and overwhelmed as their eyes open to the other side of adoption.

## Depression

In my experience talking with adoptive parents, this stage is often the most overwhelming and confusing. I can see them try to understand systemic issues while struggling with their belief in an infallible adoption system. But not being able to have something that they realize is an unattainable perfection portrayed by the media, friends, adoption agencies, and so on, is depressing. Adoptive parents really struggle to learn a way to contribute to bettering the adoption system. It can become exhausting and isolating to embrace this controversial new narrative, especially when your fellow adoptive parents are no longer on the same page.

In adoptive communities, some of the questions often heard are, "How can I prevent my child from experiencing trauma?" or "So my child will always be hurt by adoption?" There are no clear-cut answers to such questions at this time, though some may advocate for adoptions to be eliminated or for white parents not to adopt transracially. Personally, I am not anti-adoption, but I am for family preservation first. It took me a while to come to this opinion because at first I was really angry at the adoption industry. When I was adopted, no protections were in place to make sure my parents got enough education, and no one followed through to make sure my parents told me I was adopted. But after a lot of research and after numerous conversations with everyone in the adoption community, I firmly believe that adoption needs to be an option.

I also strongly believe that not enough effort is being made to keep families together when a little financial and educational support could help make that possible. However, in some situations, adoption is still the safest option for the child. The adoption industry and community does need to acknowledge, however, that currently, not enough is being done to make sure adoptive parents receive continued education and counseling in transracial adoption to help support them as their child ages. There is some focus on introductory information like haircare and navigating the adoption system, but little information is provided about identity formation, cultural immersion, and anti-racist work; this type of information needs to be prioritized.

The reality is that about 70 percent of adoptive parents are white, so the likelihood of transracial adoptions occurring is high. It can be difficult to hear all the controversial opinions that go against the very nature of white adoptive parents thinking adoption is the perfect solution. Only when you are ready to fully accept that it isn't black and white can you move on to the next stage.

## Acceptance

In my opinion, this stage is almost unattainable. To attain it, adoptive parents need to find an equilibrium where they can absorb their newfound knowledge without reacting negatively or centering themselves in apologies and commentary. This includes accepting that some parts of the system are almost impossible to change or that it will take dozens of years to make the kind of progress that those of us out of the fog want to see.

Some adoptive parents can achieve some semblance of acceptance if they work hard, but in my experience, this is often a slippery slope. Just like adoptees, the cycle of grief can often mean that adoptive parents switch back and forth between the stages. It is just a part of life. It is human instinct to protect ourselves from pain, and admitting that there are problems that you cannot fix is difficult. This is why I've only ever seen one or two adoptive parents stay in this stage for long.

# 2

# TOXIC POSITIVITY, MICROAGGRESSIONS, AND GROWING UP AS A TRANSRACIAL ADOPTEE

Over the past few years, many adoptee advocates have dedicated their time and efforts to elevating adoptees' voices in the media, blogs, adoption Facebook groups, and forums. To be honest, I was a little overwhelmed when I stumbled upon this very passionate group of advocates. They are intent on highlighting the voices of the adoption triad that seem to get pushed aside in favor of adoptive parents who have very one-sided positive takes on the adoption process.

When I first started reading some of the comments on social media from adoptees out of the fog, I originally found myself sympathizing with adoptive parents because I had believed that adoption was primarily a beautiful thing. It can be difficult to temper our own emotions when another person discusses a topic we hold so close to our hearts in a disparaging way. This was especially true for me in the beginning; I wanted to believe that when my parents adopted me, they did so with good intentions. Also, despite some difficulties in my childhood, I thought I had better upbringing than many unfortunate children in the world. I thought, who am I to go against adoption or agree with those speaking out against it when adoption had afforded me so many privileges?

So, instead of jumping into these conversations that quickly grew heated, I stayed silent, absorbed as much information as I could, and made a list of questions about topics I didn't know much about. It didn't take long before I began uncovering the darker side of adoption that no one had discussed with me before. It was only then that I could understand why some adoptees were angry—why they didn't use patience and tact when engaging with adoptive parents, but instead used blunt words that cut many to the quick.

## TOXIC POSITIVITY

According to *Psychology Today*, *toxic positivity* refers to the idea that staying positive is the only right way to live your life.[1] When I apply this idea to the adoption community, I think it refers to the overarching idea that adoption is *always* positive and that this positive light is the only proper way in which to view adoption. When the dominant narrative in adoption comes from adoptive parents, it is almost a given that this type of toxic positivity will take root and grow. Feel-good stories about adoption are always very popular; it is the more nuanced ones that typically receive criticism for diverging from the dominant narrative.

One great example is when the first adopted Black Gerber Baby was announced—an announcement that went viral all over the news, and on parenting sites in particular. The stories about this baby argued that love is the most important part of building a family. The family pictures of an adorable Black baby girl and her white adoptive parents and siblings immediately spread throughout the internet. I first saw them when they showed up as part of this feel-good story on most of my friends' Facebook pages. But, slowly, the posts reappeared in my timeline with another take on the story.

I gave a sigh of relief as I realized that I wasn't the only one uncomfortable with this narrative. As a transracial adoptee, I cringed when I saw the titles of several of these articles discussing Magnolia's new spot as the 2020 Gerber Baby, not because she wasn't the cutest baby I had seen besides my own two children, but because I knew that the news and comment section would be riddled with a savior mentality and toxic positivity.

As I dove into the comments on these Gerber Baby articles to satisfy my instinctive curiosity as an adoptee of color, I saw dozens that perpetuated the toxic positivity that plagues the adoption community. Hundreds of comments appeared from those "touched" by adoption; even those who didn't have any personal connection to adoption at all said that "Adoptions are awesome!" The consensus was that Gerber was doing an amazing thing by holding a positive platform for adoption.

Celebrating adoption is a privileged viewpoint that a lot of white adoptive parents promote. Like Courtney Earl (Magnolia's adoptive mother), they often mention that the birth parents chose life, forgetting that another option to adoption is parenting. If birth parents received more support from family, friends, and their community, they would often choose to parent their child instead of resorting to adoption. I was glad that such a beautiful baby had won the campaign, but my heart hurt for this child who had her story shared so publicly before she had a chance to be ready and to process her adoption on her own terms.

When white adoptive parents take over the narrative of an adopted child's story, who is really advocating for what is best for the child? Or what is best for the birth family? Who is considering the repercussions of oversharing the child's history before they are old enough to process their own story?

By allowing an adopted child to promote the Gerber brand when she is too young to consent, Magnolia's adoptive parents show their privileged positions. By telling her story in this way, they further promote the adoptive parent narrative that love simply makes everything easier in adoptive families. They use this press to tell us how the adoptive community rallies around them and simply mention the child's birth family almost as an afterthought.

When children are adopted, at any age, they experience the trauma of being separated from their birth family. But what about when they are adopted as infants? Is there trauma then?

In infancy and early childhood, children attach and bond with their primary caregiver; this bond can be influenced by gestation, their mother's health, and genetic vulnerabilities.[2] Mothers can differentiate their infant's smell from another baby, and babies show a strong preference for clothes worn by their moms.[3] Newborns also show a preference for their mothers compared to other caregivers, even while they are still in the womb.[4] So yes, even a newborn child can experience trauma and grief when separated from their birth mother.[5] The grief that adopted children feel is real and should be validated because it affects them their whole lives. Children who have experienced trauma or neglect experience further complications, but all adopted children grieve the loss of their biological family, heritage, and culture to some degree.[6]

Studies have found that any type of separation from parents, as the result of anything from trauma to military deployment, is very stressful for children. Such separation can lead to anxiety and acting out, even if the child has the support of family and communities as children with military parents do. When a caregiver isn't present, children undergo long-term stress that can lead to genetic changes and abnormal physiological functioning.[7] Not only are adoptees four times more likely to attempt suicide, but studies have also shown that they experience problems with mental illnesses at a higher rate than nonadopted persons.[8]

The idea that children who are adopted by loving families are better off and do not experience trauma from being separated from their biological family is deeply problematic to me as an adoptee, especially since nurses and doctors repeatedly emphasized the importance of bonding and genetic history while I was pregnant.

One of the first things that I learned when I was pregnant was about the importance of skin-to-skin contact immediately after birth. Newborn babies are placed on their mother's chest, skin to skin typically, between the mother's breasts, dressed only in a diaper, so the front of the baby's body is in direct contact with the mother's skin. This provides the infant with warmth and stimulation. Preterm newborns who have skin-to-skin contact have been found to have more stable heart rates, temperatures, and respiratory rates. Some studies show that babies at twelve months old who received skin-to-skin contact at birth are likely to perform better on development scales as well. Mothers who have this experience also report more positive maternal feelings, less depression, and more empowerment in their role as parents because the feel-good hormone, oxytocin, is released during this first contact.[9]

Because the importance of this bonding with my baby was reinforced over and over by medical professionals during my pregnancy, it simply baffles me that when it comes to adoption, these formative postpartum moments are almost pushed aside to focus on the infallible positive adoption narrative. The idea that separating a child from their first family at birth or any time after is a perfect solution without consequences is a disservice to the child, the adoptive family, and the birth family. Adoptive parents need to recognize that even a newborn can experience difficulties from being separated from their mother. If they don't acknowledge the trauma, adoptive parents cannot make informed decisions to help their child develop properly or cope with the stress trauma can cause.

The problem with this toxic positivity is that it lets us forget that race, genetics, and cultural traditions are very important pieces of our families and in our personal development. Love is important, but it is beyond essential that adoptive families learn that love also involves learning to accept that adoptees will not always view their adoption in only positive terms.

Adoptive parents also need to understand the complexity of adoptions for adoptees. For instance, an adopted child may find Mother's Day complicated because they want to celebrate their birth mother too, or they may want to know who their birth mother is. In addition, adoptive parents need to be aware of the difficulties adoptees face when dealing with medical issues. For some adoptees, family medical history is nonexistent. Many adoptees struggle with doctor's trips and questions about our family's medical histories. The lack of family information makes it a challenge for us and our doctors to look for warning signs or causes of current health problems. I have struggled with doctors being unaware of conditions that run in my biological family because my adoption was closed and because to maintain secrecy, my (adoptive) parents shared their own medical history with my doctors rather than my birth parents'.

This lack of medical history is just another hurdle that adoptees tend to deal with as they age. The lack of physical and medical health records can leave us unprepared for genetically linked health issues like cancer, diabetes, or mental illness. This worry about our family health history is ongoing and often continues after we have our own biological children when we start to worry about their health. The idea that love makes a family and that as long as you love your child, everything will be great all or most of the time does not take complications like these into account.

The work involved in raising an adopted child, especially a child of color, does not stop with giving them love. It means that adopted parents need to dive into uncomfortable situations to learn more about their adopted child's culture, to support their child through their trauma, and to love them when it's not simply about Instagram photos and Gerber prizes. Adoptees are not props. We are people, often with complex histories, that everyone often feels privileged to know. For instance, strangers can ask intrusive questions like why we were adopted, if our parents were on drugs, or if we plan to or why we searched for our birth family. Normally people wouldn't dare to ask strangers these types of personal questions, but when they find out you are adopted, they often feel entitled to ask.

## CHALLENGES MULTIRACIAL KIDS FACE

By now, you would think that racial issues would've been well on the path to being resolved. It's disappointing that, as I'm writing this book, we still have so much work to do regarding race and racism (perhaps more than we realize). Today, BIPOC still face discrimination frequently. For example, Janet Anormaliza, who lives in the town where I was raised, wrote a post on Facebook explaining how a white couple told her to "go back where she came from."[10] She is a woman of Ecuadorian descent who was born in Brooklyn in the United States. Now, this woman is not an adoptee, but this vital example demonstrates some of the racism and microaggressions your adopted child may experience through-out their life. I wish I could say Janet's story surprised me, but it didn't. I have experienced microaggressions since I was a young child and I worry about my children being subjected to these same prejudices for simply existing and going about their everyday lives. As a product of international adoption, I can say that comments like these always strike a nerve. It makes me angry when people question my citizenship because of my race and ethnicity, but it also makes me self-conscious because I never asked to come to America in the first place. I was adopted as a baby and grew up in a white family, in the middle of white suburbia. My immigrant relatives were from Italy and Portugal and were insanely proud of being Americans. I never once questioned that I was American enough until strangers told me that if I wasn't happy when I learned that I was adopted, I should leave and go back to where I came from. It hurt that simply by expressing my own experiences as a late-discovery adoptee and advocating for ethical practices in adoption, I immediately became a target for other Americans to attack.

In an anonymous survey of approximately fifty transracial adoptees I conducted online, many stated that their first experiences with racism were as children. In my transracial adoptee groups, many Asian adoptees expressed their hurt over United States President Donald Trump referring to COVID-19 as the "Kung-Flu." These are just some of the many microaggressions and experiences of racism that adoptees of color face throughout our lives. Unfortunately, many transracial adoptees also face microaggressions from our own family members who cling to a colorblind mentality. I discuss both microaggressions and color-blindness over the next few pages.

## Microaggressions and Their Impact

Transracial adoption is considered the most visible of all adoptions, and as transracial adoptees, we often feel more conscious of our race because of our parents' visible differences from us. Transracial adoptees have unique experiences as we develop our identity; together, these are referred to as the *transracial adoption paradox*. More specifically, this term refers to the set of contradictory experiences faced by adoptees who are members of racial minority groups raised by a white majority culture.[11]

The research on the relationship between mental health and discrimination of transracial adoptees is still in the beginning stages, but in 2015, a study did find that experiences with discrimination are associated with substance use issues, anxiety, and even cheating.[12] Because there are links between racial discrimination and the health of adoptees, both physical and mental, the adoption community must become more open to listening to the experiences of adult adoptees who are willing to share their struggles with the aim of educating and preparing adoptive parents for what their children may go through.

The traditional thought process is that racism involves overt acts of hate against BIPOC, but the truth is that racism often appears in more nuanced ways. In addition, research has shown that white Americans struggle to accept the more nuanced divisions of racism due to its possible implication in their involvement.[13] More subtle acts of racism are commonly known as *microaggressions*, which can also be broken up into three forms: microassaults, microinsults, and microinvalidations.

*Microassaults* are the more overt forms of discrimination; they can take the form of either verbal or nonverbal attacks or even avoidant behaviors.[14] Common examples include a white person crossing the street to avoid a BIPOC or clutching their purse on an elevator when a person of color stands next to them or when a white employee pays more attention to a BIPOC customer and follows them around the store. When this happens to transracial adoptees, and our white parents join us, the employee suddenly finds it no longer necessary to follow us.

*Microinsults* are insensitive statements or actions that put down a person's racial identity.[15] Microinsults that people of color experience are statements like, "Oh, you're pretty for a Black/Asian/Indigenous girl." Or "I thought you'd be better at math because you are Asian."

*Microinvalidations* are more common for adoptees and occur when a person negates or denies the feelings and experiences of a person of color.[16] Transracial adoptees often experience micro-invalidations when we share experiences with racism with our adoptive families that are then denied. We may be told that "I didn't mean it *that* way" or "you think everything is racist."

## Effects on Mental Health

As I said earlier, research has begun documenting the harmful effects of racism on the mental and physical health of people of color. Now we know that these effects can lead to higher rates of depression, anxiety, suicidal ideation, and even obesity and cardiovascular disease.[17] Some studies show that negative mental health symptoms can appear when people of color are treated like second-class citizens, when they are exoticized, or when they have their experiences invalidated. Racism is often a stressor that elicits coping responses as well as physical and mental stress responses that can contribute to negative health outcomes. Racial minorities can also experience a trauma response that can result in hyper-vigilance and hypersensitivity to certain social situations that are triggering. In addition, racism can contribute to negative effects on mental health when people of color internalize negative racial stereotypes that harm their self-worth. Institutional racism contributes to their experiences of the effects of chronic stressors and poor living conditions.[18] The lack of a quality support network and the limited number of health professionals and therapists of color can contribute a significant barrier to mental health access.[19]

As a woman of color, I've found that being counseled by a white therapist creates a gap in the quality of care I receive. Even if I don't add in the factor of being an adoptee, being a multiracial Latina makes it difficult for me to receive quality care from trained professionals because they are not familiar with my family dynamic and do not have similar experiences with racism. After ten years and several different therapists, I finally found a therapist who is a woman of color; I had to give up on finding one who was also adoption competent in favor of keeping one who understood my experiences as a woman of color.

In 2016, approximately 85 percent of therapists in the United States were white. Only 4 percent were Black, and another 4 percent were Hispanic.[20] If you want to seek out a therapist who is also adoption competent, you will find very few, and those who are available may not be in your network. This creates a huge discrepancy in the quality and frequency of care people of color are able to receive, which is why it should not be surprising that racism is a significant risk factor of negative mental health outcomes.[21]

Adoptees of color who are raised by white adoptive parents are often also raised in primarily white areas and have minimal contact with other people of color, making them highly aware of their different status as a person of color. Older adoptees, in particular, report more encounters with racism in addition to feeling uncomfortable with being a different race than their peers. Studies on transracial adoptive families rarely focus on the importance of helping transracial adoptees cope with racism. In one of the few studies that focused on Korean adoptees, it was reported that their adoptive parents are often ill-equipped to deal with such issues.[22]

At some point, transracial adoptees may hear their parents say something racially insensitive. For example,

*Those people.*

or

*I can't understand them. He's Chinese or something, you know one of those. I don't know which kind.*

When it comes to these occasions, when adoptive parents slip up and say things like this, transracial adoptees are left with empty pits in our stomachs; we question whether we should point out how what they're saying is wrong or whether doing so will just turn negative attention on us. We wonder:

*Will Mom be upset if I tell her that's kind of racist?*

*If my parents say things like this about other people of color . . . what do they think about me? Or my birth family?*

*Why am I different?*

Moments like these can be almost inconsequential for white adoptive parents who do not necessarily realize that what they are saying is a microaggression. But at the root of it, these kinds of statements are proof to their adopted children that despite how often our adoptive parents may say that they do not see color, they do. Adoptees' development can be impacted by their parents' lived experiences as people in a racial majority and the racial biases that the parents may be unintentionally perpetuating.

The difference between raising a child of color in a white majority home versus raising a child of color in a home of the same race is complex. Although well-intentioned white adoptive parents are often eager to incorporate their adopted child's culture and ethnic background into their lives, they often miss the mark. For instance, such white parents may avoid discussing racism and favor parenting with a colorblind mentality, unlike in Black homes, where parents provide their children with racial socialization and teach their children what to expect from Black people and white people. The lessons that white adoptive parents teach their adopted children of color may unintentionally perpetuate racial discrepancies due to their experiences of privilege.[23]

# COLORBLINDNESS AND ITS REPERCUSSIONS

When it first became popular for white parents to adopt children of color, families were advised to raise adoptees of color as if they were white. This recommendation was based on the idea that recognizing racial differences would negatively affect development. Later research has shown that transracial adoptees are not exempt from prejudice and racial stress simply because they were raised within a white family.[24] In an ideal world, children would not face any discrimination. Unfortunately, we live in a world that emphasizes our physical appearance, and often that includes our race and ethnicity.

Racial prejudice is a pressing issue. By age three, children can identify racial groups; by ages six to eight, children can consistently classify others by race.[25] Despite this, many adopted parents raised children with a colorblind mentality. *Colorblindness*, also known as the *colorblind racial ideology*, is the widely held belief that skin color does not play a role in interpersonal interactions and institutional policies and/or practices.[26] As a woman of color, it is hard for me to understand why so many adoptive parents take a colorblind perspective when race plays a significant role in so many things.

For example, people of color have higher rates of poverty, unemployment, and incarceration. Latinx individuals make up around 23 percent of the prison population whereas Black individuals make up 33 percent. If we assume the prison population is representative of the population at large, logically this doesn't seem to make sense because white Americans make up about 64 percent of the United States population and only 30 percent of the prison population. The math doesn't add up.[27] Why do Black and Latinx Americans make up a larger segment of the prison population when white Americans are the majority population in our country? Also consider health inequalities. Black infant mortality rates are twice that of non-Hispanic white infants, and Black people are more likely to die from a stroke or heart disease before the age of seventy-five than their white counterparts. Latinx and Black individuals also have higher rates of diabetes, tuberculosis, HIV, and preventable hospitalizations.[28]

As adopted children grow up, they also become increasingly aware of racism and discrimination in their day-to-day lives. The loss of cultural socialization has correlated with decreasing self-worth and increasing depressive symptoms, particularly for those who were confused about their ethnic and racial identity.[29]

One way to combat this is to embrace *cultural socialization*— the way parents address racial and ethnic issues within the family and how they communicate customs, cultural values, and behaviors to their children. In transracial adoptive families, this means transmitting the child's birth culture, which is important to creating a strong ethnic identity and overall well-being.[30] Doing this is not a clear-cut process as it is in same-race families. This may be because white Americans are less likely to consider themselves part of a racial group; this can contribute to the difficulty they have recognizing the privilege in their lives and can make it easier for white adoptive parents to minimize or even deny the significance of race in our society.[31]

Parents who subscribe less to colorblindness seem to engage more with post-adoption support groups and cultural activities and even speak about racism with their adopted children. However, studies show that it is best to participate in cultural socialization in addition to engaging in racial awareness. Parents who are willing to put in the extra effort to learn about racism and discrimination are more likely to positively contribute to their child's ethnic development and well-being.[32]

When adoptive parents find it difficult to believe adoptees when we try to share our experiences with racism, it can cause conflicts in our relationships. As transracial adoptees, we are in a unique position to be deeply involved in our adoptive parents' majority culture while also being part of a minority culture that is subjected to discrimination and racism. Adoptees may find it painful to navigate the space between these two very different cultures while trying to fit in with each, especially if they don't have a definitive way to merge the two without repercussions and difficulty. It can be painful to see our adoptive parents' jealousy when we express interest in our birth culture, and this may make us feel guilty, and at the same time, we may experience overwhelming shame that we don't know our birth culture well enough.

Another unique complication for transracial adoptees is that we experience an umbrella of white privilege when we are with our white adoptive family that protects us, but the second we are out on our own and do not have our adoptive families around to vouch for us, we lose that protection; at this point, we must be prepared for the social implications of being a BIPOC. If we are raised in homes that promote colorblindness, we can be left vulnerable and unprepared for the reality of our position in a country built on systemic racism.

In my experience as a mixed-race adoptee, having conversations with my parents about the racism and microaggressions I have experienced as a woman of color has often left me feeling frustrated and hurt. I was taught growing up that if I worked hard enough in life, my color wouldn't matter. I could accomplish anything. But at the same time, I am treated differently by others because I am Latina, and when my parents dismissed that my race was the reason, it left me feeling gaslighted. When I worked at my father's restaurant, customers would treat me as the uneducated help. It confused me when they changed their tune when they found out I was the Italian owner's daughter.

My parents' colorblind view did not protect me when I was out on my own. The world viewed me as a woman of color and treated me as such. Having white parents protected me when I was a child, but as I matured and went off to college or to work, my interactions in my day-to-day life were those of a woman of color. At times when I was shopping I would be followed around by staff, and on more than one occasion, a cop cornered me and tried to get me to admit I was guilty of a crime.

One occasion that stands out to me was on a particularly long drive back to my college campus during my junior year after one of my breaks. I liked to drive in the evening when traffic was not an issue. On this occasion, I was pulled over by an officer two hours into the drive. I had not been speeding, my tags and license were all in order, and I had my seat belt on. The officer questioned me for a long time, asking me where I was coming from and where I was going. Despite his aggressive manner, I remained calm, and he eventually let me go with an excuse that my headlights seemed extra bright. Naturally, I was shaken up by the experience and couldn't help but notice the difference between it and the polite exchanges my parents or my white-passing boyfriend experienced each time they were pulled over. It was apparent that I was being profiled, and when I tried to discuss this with my parents, they maintained that my color didn't matter—the officer was simply doing his job.

I tried to discuss these experiences with my parents many times, but they would act shocked that people would do the things that they had done and make excuses for their behavior; it made me feel like I imagined the discrimination. Finding myself in the position of educating my parents about racism was exhausting. I would put in many hours of emotional labor, finding examples of racism in our community, the news, and my life, only to be shut down. It was only after I joined the adoptee community that I realized my experience with my family was not rare.

When Black children and other children of color are adopted, it does not exempt them from dealing with racism and discrimination. Most adopted children of color live isolated from their birth culture, and many do not have an opportunity to connect on a personal level with others of the same race until their parents take them to cultural camps. Even there, the children are often also transracial adoptees who have some trouble identifying with their birth culture.[33] Adoptive parents can struggle with how much culture their adopted children should keep and often view introducing such culture as a parenting decision rather than the child's birthright. Those parents who do may make attempts to embrace their child's birth culture often do so only at a surface level.

The act of incorporating multicultural books, cultural traditions, and recipes from the child's birth culture almost takes on the essence of *cultural tourism*—the selective appropriation and consumption of cultural symbols, events, and artifacts. The impact of this more superficial attempt to incorporating a child's birth culture instead of actually having an integrated life experience can make it difficult for adoptees to fully immerse themselves in their birth culture. When combined with *cultural keeping* (the cultural socialization of children that retains native group identity), cultural tourism can put adopted children of color at risk of failing to establish a collective identity or proper membership in either their birth culture or their adoptive culture, which is why it is essential that adoptive parents make consistent and authentic measures to connect their whole family with their child's birth culture.[34] Although it can be overwhelming to teach your child of color about a culture you are not as familiar with, it is your responsibility to make ongoing efforts, not just surface-level attempts like ordering takeout from your favorite Indian or Chinese restaurant.

Some great resources and activities to help you do this can be found in Chapter 9.

## IDENTITY PROBLEMS

When children start to grow up and come of age, they also typically begin to develop a strong sense of identity. But what makes up a person's identity? From birth, a child's gender roles, history, relationships, and culture all help them form their own personal identity. During adolescence, teenagers' identity formation, decision-making, and coping strategies start to become independent from their parents, allowing for self-exploration.[35] Although we know that race is a social construct based on a person's physical characteristics, it is vital to acknowledge that people's biases toward people of color also have serious and often long-term ramifications.[36]

Research has found that having an ethnic identity is essential to developing self-identity in ethnic minorities. *Ethnic identification* is a process in which individuals learn to recognize their membership in racial groups and start to internalize particular traits associated with the group into their own self-identity. This concept focuses on the psychological implications of someone's commitment to their cultural heritage, allowing a person to feel close to thoughts, feelings, and actions that tend to be part of their own culture.[37]

Different stages are involved in developing a child's ethnic identity. During the first stage, *diffusion/foreclosure*, children begin to recognize race and ethnicity. The second stage, *moratorium*, is when early adolescents (around twelve years old) explore how they personally relate to their racial or ethnic group. The final stage, *achieved ethnic identity*, culminates with an individual understanding of culture-specific traditions, customs, and world view.[38]

Just in my day-to-day experience, I have found solid ground on which to stand to connect with biracial and multiracial individuals, like my husband, because they understand how it feels to struggle to fit into two or more different cultures. Poston's biracial identity development model helps me illustrate that biracial individuals experience conflict and periods of maladjustment while they are developing their identity. From my own experience, and from discussions I have had with other transracial adoptees, I have noticed how the biracial model can closely resemble similar experiences that we face as adoptees of color. Here are the five stages of Poston's biracial identity development model.[39]

1. **Personal Identity:** This stage occurs during childhood when the child is not aware of their mixed heritage.

2. **Choice of Group Categorization:** This stage occurs when the child is pressured to choose one racial category due to the influences of parents, peers, community, and society.

3. **Enmeshment/Denial:** In this stage, individuals feel disloyal and even guilty for choosing one racial identity over another.

4. **Appreciation:** In this stage, individuals explore other racial groups and can learn to appreciate them as well.

5. **Integration:** The person may identify more with one group and appreciates the integration of their multiple racial identities.

To further explain the importance of this model and how it relates to transracial adoption, I'm going to briefly go over my own experience with each stage. My timeline is a little different than many transracial adoptees due to my late-discovery adoption, but generally, I feel like this model and these stages have helped me and will help other adoptees of color identify where they are at in terms of their identity development. Adoptive parents might also find understanding these stages helpful; when they are familiar with them, parents may find this understanding helps them show empathy for their children and perhaps even assist their children by encouraging them to explore and understand their complex identity.

Here is an example of my path through these stages:

1. **Personal Identity:** I was unaware of my race and its importance until I was nineteen due to the secrecy of my adoption.

2. **Choice of Group Categorization:** After I found out I was adopted, I was overwhelmed, surrounded by white family, friends, and community, which made it difficult for me to identify as a multiracial Latina. At the time, it was easier to identify as Italian, like my adoptive parents.

3. **Enmeshment/Denial:** During this stage, I was in college, finally surrounded by a more diverse peer group that included a strong Latinx population. It was at this time that I felt the urge to learn more about my culture, but I ended up feeling too awkward and disloyal to my family to fully dig into my roots.

4. **Appreciation:** In college, I made concrete steps to work at learning more about my identity. I started listening to Latinx music and watching shows like *Jane the Virgin* that incorporated Latinx representation. Finally, I felt an appreciation for Latinx culture even though I wasn't fully immersed in it.

5. **Integration:** I am finally comfortable identifying as a multiracial Latina and am also comfortable with

my cultural upbringing as Italian. I am successfully incorporating the Spanish language in my day-to-day life with my sons. Also, I have reached a good balance of appreciating and incorporating traditions from my adoptive parents' culture as well. To me, this looks like a diverse menu at Thanksgiving that includes empanadas and lasagna, or family parties where my grandparents speaking to me in Italian while I play Reggaetón music in the background.

Feelings of belonging can be nurtured when we engage in cultural activities, traditions, practices, and customs with others of the same race. Not surprisingly, studies have found that transracial adoptees naturally develop a bicultural identity due to their family's unique structure, allowing them to relate to their adoptive parent's culture and their own birth culture. Sometimes adoptees relate more with their adoptive families' culture or sometimes they can feel excluded by both.[40] In my personal experience, I have found it easier to relate to my family's Italian culture than to my Colombian roots because of what I was exposed to every day while growing up in a white adoptive family. As an adult, I've found that I struggle to connect to and learn about my Colombian roots because I fear rejection, because I do not know enough, and because I'm embarrassed for not knowing things I feel that I should. After all, it's a part of my identity.

*Racial-ethnic socialization* is the process of socializing children within their own race or ethnicity, encouraging racial-ethnic pride, and teaching children of color how to cope with racism, discrimination, and racial oppression. Parents who do not practice this may not have received education about racial-ethnic socialization, its importance, and how to implement it in a healthy way. Some parents may not even be aware of their own biases against other cultures, making this type of socialization even more difficult to enact. Some ways to begin this type of socialization for your adopted child include having friends of the same race as your child, embracing your child's cultural beliefs, educating yourselves and them about racial discrimination, and living in racially diverse areas.[41]

I feel that it is also essential to discuss Janet E. Helms's model for *white racial development*, due to the impact that white adoptive parents have on their adopted children of color. If white parents are unable to embrace their own racial identity, how can they teach their children the importance of embracing their ethnic identity?

The six-stage process is as follows:[42]

1. **Contact:** Obliviousness to one's whiteness and the implications of racial-group differences. Generally, this stage means you adhere to a colorblind mentality.

2. **Disintegration:** Confusion and guilt are at the forefront because you have become consciously aware of your membership and identity as a white person and the moral dilemmas that come with it.

3. **Reintegration:** Your blame-the-victim attitude is dominant, and even when you admit that white privilege exists, you may feel that it is because people of color deserve it.

4. **Pseudo-independence:** Generally, in this stage you do not feel that whites deserve privileges but you still look to people of color to confront racism rather than being actively nonracist yourself.

5. **Immersion/Emersion:** You make an effort to develop a meaningful and moral definition of whiteness and connecting to your own white identity while also working toward being actively anti-racist.

**6. Autonomy:** You reach this last stage when you are finally able to have a positive racial identity with your whiteness as well as actively pursue social justice.

Looking at these stages can be confusing, overwhelming, and, from my own personal experience and, as I recall, when I was introduced to this model in my counseling class during my undergrad for psychology, frustrating. At the time, I still was unaware of my adoption and identity as a woman of color. For the class, I had to examine and discuss where I was in the process of determining my identity. I struggled to label and admit my own personal biases and I actually felt defensive at being labeled as white. To me, what I was didn't matter, and it wasn't until I found out that I was adopted and a woman of color that I realized how important racial identity was.

I know this is a complicated example, but it allows me to truly empathize with the process that adoptive parents go through. Since I, too, once believed that I was part of a majority, race at the time didn't really hold much weight to me. I could brush it off because it didn't affect me since I had my family's whiteness to protect me when other people treated me rudely because they assumed I was Latina. But when the umbrella of whiteness was gone, I was unable to stay ignorant of the effect that race has in our society; I no longer had that protection from my parents. For white adoptive parents, it can be difficult to understand the importance of race in their transracially adopted children's lives until they understand their own racial identity. This is why I am urging adoptive parents who are looking at this model to really consider each stage and ask themselves these questions:

1. Where do I currently fit into Helms's white racial development model?

2. Where do I want to be? And why?

3. What are five concrete steps I can take to get there?

4. What are some challenges I am apt to face on the way? What can I do to make getting where I want to be easier?

Once you are able to discuss these questions openly and honestly, I believe you can better understand and empathize with your children of color. Understanding your own racial identity is a difficult process on its own, but raising children of another race and teaching them how to understand their own identities adds another complex layer. You can manage it, however, if you are willing to do the work and ask for guidance from your child's Latinx, Black, Indigenous community that you have worked to create a relationship with.

# DNA TESTING

Many adoptees, particularly those of us who had closed adoptions, often reach a point in our lives when we consider DNA testing by companies like 23andMe or Ancestry.com. The promise of concrete knowledge about our race/ethnicity, as well as possible connections to close biological relatives, is often too tempting for us to resist. Trying to establish a family medical history is a driving factor for many adoptees; I wanted to find out any medical information I could about my birth family. Using testing companies like this is often the most affordable and easily accessible option that we have.

In a *closed adoption* the adoptive family and birth family share little or no contact with one another and identifying information from the birth family typically remains confidential. Non-identifying information that is often provided to adoptive parents includes the date and place of the adoptee's birth, the age of the birth parents, and a general physical description (i.e., eye and hair color), race/ethnicity/religion of birth parents, educational level and occupation of biological parents, and the reason the child was placed.[43] Many adoptees in closed adoptions have access to little to no medical information other than basic information about their health at birth; other adoptees may have one or two lines of information that a social worker was able to ask the birth mother before the adoption was finalized.

## THINGS TO CONSIDER

The reasons that adoptees may desire a DNA search can vary from wanting medical information, to learning about their ancestry/nationality, to wanting to find biological relatives. Although such searches can open many doors, you may want to consider some things before taking tests with such companies.

For example, not only might your private information be shared, but you also might uncover some long-buried family secrets. For example, a person may take a DNA test expecting one result only to find out new information about their race and ethnicity. This can be shocking to learn after many years of growing up with a different identity. It is also important to remember that there are some barriers to access. For instance, tests can be expensive and may only be accessible in certain states and countries. In addition, not all tests provide the same information and some platforms are easier to use than others. When considering genetic testing, keep these factors in mind before deciding to move forward.

Adoptees should also make sure they don't have false expectations. Having some answers about your DNA won't necessarily fix everything, nor should you hope that you will find close birth relatives immediately once your results are in. For years after taking a 23andMe test, I held my breath every time I received an email stating that new DNA matches had been found, only to be disappointed when I found that they were distant cousins who had no information about my birth mother.

It is also important to note that results from at-home DNA kits can vary greatly. Ethnicity at a regional level is pretty accurate, but more specific levels of analysis are less precise. Health information should also be taken with a grain of salt because false-positive results for the BRCA1 or BRCA2 gene mutations are not uncommon. That said, your results, in conjunction with any history you know about your birth family, can help you make medical decisions down the line.[44] According to a certified genetic counselor, DNA testing from consumer testing companies is often just a good place to start if you're interested in discovering more information about your genetic risks. It can provide small insights but it is unlikely to provide you with meaningful information about your possible health risks.[45]

## LANGUAGE

When you adopt a child of color, particularly via international adoption, the child's birth culture often speaks a different language than the culture of your adoptive family. Some adoptive parents make efforts to learn and teach their adopted children about these things, but many do not.

Research has shown that internationally adopted children do not fit into the existing categories of bilingual language learning; the majority of children adopted internationally lose their bilingual status because their adoptive families are unable to maintain their birth language. What typically occurs is *arrested language development* in the adoptee—the premature stop of the growth of the child's birth language—as the adoptee develops their adopted language, leaving the child at risk for the failure to develop dual proficiency in either language.[46] Language loss is often observed in immigrants of all ages, but that speed of the loss in international adoptees is significant due to three factors: 1) their low level of first language skills; 2) their lack of motivation for retaining their first language and their lack of opportunity to practice; and 3) their lack of support for their first language in their adoptive family or community at large.[47]

For example, Russian children who are adopted between the ages of four and eight often lose their native expressive language within three to six months of their adoption, and they typically lose all functional use of their birth language within a year of adoption. Infants and toddlers typically lose function of the birth language faster.[48] However, another study of Dutch adults who were adopted internationally from Korea found that children who were adopted between three to five months of age had a learning advantage from early exposure to a different language in their first half of life that left traces that may make it easier for them to relearn the language later on.[49]

Research has also found that many international adoptees have negative emotional reactions to hearing their birth language, which increases the risk of language loss over time.[50] Language has long since been identified as a powerful trigger for posttraumatic stress disorder, often because it is a representation of a person's life history. And adoptees, particularly older adoptees who have had traumatic pasts in orphanages or who have suffered abuse, can be triggered by their birth language. For other adoptees seeking to connect with their adoptive families and community, forgetting the language can have many immediate positive consequences by helping them blend in.[51]

When I started to dig into my identity as a Colombian adoptee, one of the biggest issues I had was not knowing the language of my birth culture. I had spent most of my life up to that point learning Italian, my adoptive father's language, from classes in school and interactions with family members. I had even learned some Portuguese in order to communicate with my grandmother on my adoptive mom's side. But I had not learned Spanish, the language I had heard for nine months in my birth mother's womb and for several months after in the orphanage. I knew less Spanish than most of my white friends, and I knew less than my adoptive parents.

Not knowing the language, while most people around me knew at least a little Spanish made me angry, resentful, and depressed. I hated that my parents, who knew Spanish, put their desires before what would have been best for me. They placed their culture and language in a place of higher importance in our family, even after I expressed a desire to learn Spanish. They did not attempt to help me learn, did not attempt to speak Spanish around me, and even expressed annoyance when I would listen to music in Spanish, as I tried to express interest in my culture. My attempts at home to sing or say simple Spanish phrases were looked down upon, and I was put under pressure to speak Italian around them instead.

## Judgment

When I began meeting other Latinos, not being able to speak Spanish became a stressor on those relationships. A lot of Latinx in the United States speak Spanish, and passing judgment on those who don't is common, especially from the older generation. There's an expectation that in order to be a part of the culture and respect it, Latinos need to speak the language. Latinx who are adopted are often put in an awkward position when we are approached by others who just assume we speak the language. Sometimes we are met with anger, even pity, and, ultimately, the situation makes us feel othered. Even adoptees who speak or understand the language can be teased for our American accents, our slow pace, or our refusal to answer in Spanish.

When I was growing up, my adoptive parents emphasized Italian and Portuguese so when I discovered my adoption, I felt

I was missing a big part of myself by not knowing much of my first language. Because my parents spoke multiple languages after learning to adapt when they immigrated to the United States, I was fortunate enough to at least understand some Italian and Portuguese. But when I started to actively learn Spanish, I was met by a block of shame that I couldn't seem to break through. I struggled with being embarrassed when I pronounced words wrong, with remembering tenses, and with a lot of anger. I felt as if it was my fault that I didn't know the language. That because of my blood and because I was born in Colombia, I should have already known the language, and my trouble learning it made me feel as if I had failed somehow.

I refused to speak Spanish with any friends or family who spoke the language. My self-esteem tanked every time I stumbled on a word. I thought that when others assumed I knew the language and then found out I was adopted, they would look at me with pity. Now, of course my situation isn't the case with all of us. Some adoptees may be received with open arms when they begin their journey of integrating into their own culture, and some may not. But I know that my experience is common because I've talked with many adoptees on my podcast and in adoption groups who have also experienced a mental block. Sometimes this block is so strong that it makes me nervous about using language learning apps to practice; it even makes me feel anxious about taking classes.

This is why it is important to discuss these barriers—because as an adoptee, like me, you may feel self-conscious about negative emotions that may surface when you take classes in your birth language, or when you try to participate in other cultural activities, like martial arts, or even certain religious activities. For example, I tried to join a Spanish class in college but did not have the option to join the beginner class because I was Latina and the teacher wouldn't sign off on me joining since she assumed I had some knowledge of the language. Eventually, when I tried online classes, I saw that none of the other students were Latinx and felt shame and self-loathing because they knew more about the language than I did. This shame clung to me like a second skin and made it difficult for me to learn the language because of the constant negative emotions I felt and still feel when taking classes. For me, it wasn't worth the time and effort when I would get stuck in a spiral of negative self-talk anytime I attempted a class.

Years of research supports the idea that language expresses, symbolizes, and embodies cultural reality, meaning that identity and language are often tied together. *Heritage language* (a language associated with one's cultural background) is often a significant aspect of ethnic identity for immigrant families. Research has also found that adoptive parents often pursue heritage language for three main reasons: 1) their children look like their birth culture, and they realize that society will often expect their adopted children to know their birth language based on their appearance alone; 2) adult adoptees recommend that new adoptive parents make efforts to teach their children their birth language and these parents are eager to avoid making the perceived mistakes other adoptive parents have made; and 3) adopted children expressed interest in learning their heritage language.[52]

Adoptive parents may find choosing a course of action confusing. On the one hand, adult adoptees often say that the best thing to do is encourage your adopted children to learn about their culture and to engage in those activities with them. But on the other hand, these activities may result in pain and trauma, which is often underdiscussed. There is no perfect course of action to take.

Teaching your children to embrace their birth language and culture is complex. It is important to use lots of encouragement and sometimes even therapy to help your child work through everything. It can even seem counterproductive to put your child in language classes when they tell you they hate them. I've talked to many adoptees who wish that their parents had made them stick with learning their birth language as kids because they are now adults who feel as if they've missed out on that experience.

What is most important, however, is that you communicate openly with your child and their care team (if a therapist is involved) and come up with a game plan together. One year your child might not be ready to delve into language classes, and the next, they may. You may find that once they are a bit older or more involved with other adoptees in the adoptee community, they may have the support they need to dig into their heritage language. They may even want you along on that journey so they can have someone they love practice with them.

As long as you communicate openly with your child or adult adoptee, you can work together on how to approach language development. If you are adoptive parents of younger children, I suggest that the entire family learn the child's birth language from the day the child joins the family. In fact, some studies show that white adoptive moms have started to view learning their child's birth language as a requirement for positive racial identity; they view it as a burden that parents should share with their adoptive children and as a positive way for the child to connect with the birth or foster family.[53] There are many benefits to becoming bilingual, but for adoptees, having the ability to communicate in our birth language is often a gift we will cherish, especially if our adoptive families are supportive and involved in the process.

## Code-Switching

Another facet of language development that is important for adoptive families to learn about is *code-switching*, which is the mixed use of two or more languages and also the way you express yourself and adapt to different social situations.[54] For many Latinx people, this can involve switching between English and Spanish to communicate depending on what situation they find themselves in, and for many Black individuals, this can include switching from their natural hair to more "corporate" approved styles at work or switching from English to African American Vernacular English (AAVE). Code-switching can look different depending on the cultural group a person is a part of, and it is essential for adoptive parents to learn, understand, and embrace their child as they develop this ability.

Code-switching is often prevalent because of the expectations and standards of the dominant culture. If you consider your neighborhood and community, you are part of what defines the common attributes of people in this group. What language do you speak? How do you dress? How do you greet one another? When considering the dominant narrative, it is important to note that the dominant culture is often perceived by society as more "normal," "good," or even "successful."[55]

One prominent example of code-switching in the media was a video of President Barack Obama in 2012. The video went viral because of the clear difference in how he greeted the white assistant coach versus the Black NBA player, Kevin Durant. For those who are unfamiliar with the clip, President Obama shook the white coach's hand in a professional manner but embraced the NFL player in a more familiar handshake and half hug. In this example, the code-switching was in the physical way the President changed his behaviors based on who he was interreacting with.[56]

When I think of my personal experience with code-switching, I am very aware of what my family perceives as proper manners and language. Anything other than that is often met with criticism, which has made it harder for me to connect with other Latinos or people of color who are surrounded by more family and friends who can code-switch in the same way. When I am around my Latino family and friends, I naturally slip into a more relaxed dialect and use Spanish words in my speech along with slang. And on the occasions I forget to switch back with my adoptive family, I am immediately criticized for how I am talking and acting. In fact, on more than one occasion, my mother has asked, "Do you talk like that to your coworkers?" This question and tone of voice make me aware that the way I am talking and acting is seen as less than and immediately fills me with shame.

As a woman of color, I am very aware of the impact that the way that I speak, look, and act has on how I am treated in the world, especially in the workforce. It can be painful for adopted children of color to realize this when adoptive parents, like my own, make statements or use body language that portrays their dislike, or even sometimes disdain, for our code-switching. Learning how to code-switch and embrace mannerisms that help me connect with other Latinos is important not only for my self-esteem but for my cultural development. If I am able to connect more with my language and mannerisms, I am less likely to be othered and even pitied for being adopted. This is why it is important for the adoptive parents of children of color to realize the impact their inflections and words have on their children.

Sometimes adoptees struggle to be recognized by others in our birth culture and notice our parents' reactions to our behavior change. Adoptive parents should encourage code-switching because it is an essential part of being a person of color in a white-dominant society. This behavior allows us to connect with others like us in our various communities while also maintaining "proper" appearances while we are at school or work. Adoptive parents who are nervous about code-switching need only to think about how their own speech and behavior patterns change the moment they are home, in their sweats, or the difference in the way they speak and act when they go to a party with close friends versus when they attend a work meeting with the CEO of their company. Humans are incredibly skilled at adapting to certain social situations, and your children will learn to master the skills of code-switching over time. The more support you show, the easier it will be for them.

*AUTHOR'S NOTE The issues covered in this chapter may require the assistance of a licensed therapist, mentoring by adoption-competent professionals, or further research and reflection. You can find a list of resources in Chapter 9 as well as activities to improve dialogue within your adoptive family and to improve your personal growth as an adoptive parent.*

# 3

# A HISTORY OF
# TRANSRACIAL ADOPTION AND
# THE ADOPTION INDUSTRY

**W**hen adoptive parents are faced with the question of why they chose to adopt, they often say it is because adoption is in their hearts, or that they felt it was God's path for them, but when it comes down to it, one of the biggest factors is fertility. And I think it is important that this fact is spoken about. As a woman who has faced infertility, I know the struggles of surgeries and pills, and at the end of the day, it is nothing to be ashamed of. But that doesn't make it okay to pressure other women to choose adoption or to stop other couples from adopting based on your beliefs.

According to the CDC, women prefer to adopt a single child, without siblings, who is younger than two years old and does not have disabilities. Most women looking to adopt are of higher incomes, married, and have attempted fertility treatments, and many are surgically sterile or have some problems with fertility.

The data show the opposite is true for men. Men who adopt are likely to have fathered children before and not to have used infertility services.[1] It is interesting that many fathers who have biological children choose to adopt later, not for fertility reasons but often because women tend to gain custody of children in divorces allowing their new male partners more opportunities to adopt.[2]

I have noticed a few things having to do with prospective adoptive parents' priorities regarding their adoption process. Some of the top ones I have seen discussed over and over in adoption groups I have joined in my search for more understanding are these:

1. The speed of the process

2. The cost, including fees for home study, lawyers, travel, and so on

3. Whether to foster or adopt domestically or internationally

Each time I see adoptive parents focus on money, speed, and type of adoption, it blows my mind that they don't think much about the history and ethics of the adoption system. It seems that this is because the adoption industry focuses on making sure agencies follow a profitable business model rather than an ethical one.

In January of 2020, a bill passed in Tennessee that made it legal for adoption agencies to refuse prospective adoptive parents who were in same-sex relationships as long as doing so violated the agency's written religious convictions, moral convictions, or policies.[3] Because of the "need" for more stable and healthy families for children in the foster care system, it seems odd that government officials would allow agencies to discriminate against couples based on their LGBTQ+ identity, especially since more states have started to pass similar measures.

Each year approximately 140,000 adoptions are finalized in the United States; the demand for white infants exceeds the supply, while leaving more older children of color in foster care.[4] In fact, since the 1970s, countries have seen a widening gap between couples wishing to adopt and the actual number of children who are available for adoption. In Italy, there are approximately fifteen couples for every local child available for adoption; in the United States, only one out of three women who seek to adopt succeed; and similar rates are seen in Singapore and France. The decrease in infants available in developed countries can be linked with societal changes in these countries that have reduced the stigma of single women raising children and low-cost and easily accessible access to birth control. This drop-off is why international adoptions have become a significant means of finding adoptable children, where access to birth control and safe abortions can be difficult to obtain.[5]

Historically, adoptions in the United States have been based on "matching" children to adoptive parents to uphold racially homogenous families.[6] State laws that govern part of adoption processes and are not monitored by any federal agency allow a free-market dynamic that focuses on supply and demand.[7] Reports of primarily Black or mixed-race children being adopted *from* the United States to Canada, England, Spain, Italy, and France started appearing in 2004.[8] But if over a million couples are looking to adopt in the United States, why are children being adopted into other countries? Because the majority of prospective white adoptive parents, who make up 70 percent of adopters, prefer to adopt white children.

There is a racial hierarchy defined as *colorism* where lighter skin is preferred over darker.[9] Colorism is alive and well in the adoption process and industry. Agencies have been shown to charge adoptive parents a higher fee to adopt a white infant than to adopt a Black infant. The majority of adoptions of white infants occur domestically and can range from $4,000 to $30,000, whereas the adoption costs of Black children, who are primarily adopted from foster care, range from $0 to $2,500. When you look at children considered "closer to white" that are available through international adoption from preferred countries like China, Russia, Guatemala, Korea, and Romania, the costs range from $7,000 to $25,000—further evidence of colorism.[10]

Children can be lumped into categories that best fit the adoption industry. Some even categorize children based on their proximity to whiteness and whether they can be considered honorary white due to a history of assimilation in America. Some of the countries that are often considered honorary white in international adoption agencies include China, Korea, India, Taiwan, Japan, Thailand, and Mexico.[11] Another category listed in agency reports/options includes darker-skinned Latinos and Southeast Asians, often referred to collectively as Black. Some of the countries in this category include Cambodia, the Philippines, Vietnam, Haiti, Ethiopia, Nigeria, Liberia.[12]

This might be a bit confusing, so let me break it down a little. As we have discussed before, agencies know that there is often a demand for white babies and children. Due to that demand, they label children according to their proximity to whiteness based on adoptive parents' trends and preferences. So, although adoptive parents may be open to adopting a child of color, many show preferences for adopting mixed-race children or other children of color who are closer to passing as white. When agencies cater to this desire and set up their categories, it's not just a coincidence that they can charge more adoption fees for such preferences.

For the past few years, most international adoptions have come from primarily white countries or ones that are considered honorary white, with the exception of Guatemala. The high adoption rate there can be attributed to its more liberal adoption policies allowing for older couples, single people, and gay adoptive parents.[13] When you look at the numbers as an adoptee and then try to fit this information with the voices of adoptive parents who have repeated that "race does not matter" and "love makes a family," it is hard to dispel the cognitive dissonance that these two factors invoke.

The *theory of cognitive dissonance* refers to the psychological discomfort that individuals feel when faced with conflicting beliefs, behaviors, or attitudes. When applied to the adoption industry and the way adoptive parents react when faced with the nuances and sometimes ethical issues of the process, we can see how the need to reduce dissonance can pressure them to avoid certain hard truths like the trauma in adoption.[14] *Cognitive dissonance* refers to the discomfort we feel as a result of holding two beliefs, attitudes, or conflicting values. For example, many adoptive parents believe that adoption is beautiful and saves children from a worse fate, but more are becoming aware of the impact of systemic racism and now may also believe that some ethical problems crop up with adoption, all of which can cause cognitive dissonance.

Some ways people work to ease the discomfort of cognitive dissonance are the following: 1) they change their behavior to bring it more in line with the opposing belief; 2) they justify the behavior by changing one of their beliefs; 3) and they develop new beliefs to help justify their behavior.[15] And when you look at the dominant belief in the adoption industry, that "love makes a family and color doesn't matter," you can see the need to justify why agencies and adoptive parents make their preferences of an adopted child's race/ethnicity known.

How can we believe the voices of our adoptive families when they tell us they don't see color when so much evidence shows us that race does matter? Race factors into the decisions adoptive parents make from the moment they fill out the adoption paperwork. Right from the start, they are able to choose whether or not they are open to adopting a Black child, a mixed-race baby, or other children that are BIPOC. From the moment a parent chooses adoption, they have the choice to choose race . . . because it does matter to adoptive families—so much so that US-born Black and mixed-race babies are being adopted to countries like Canada, where birth parents in the United States may think racism is less of an issue due to agencies that are starting to require courses to heighten racial sensitivity.[16]

Why do agencies ask potential adoptive parents about their preferences? Why do more white couples prefer mixed-race children? The adoption community justifies these preferences to reduce the discomfort they and adoptive parents feel of their belief that race doesn't matter. The evidence showing that a child's race and ethnicity is important to adoptive parents makes it apparent that color does matter. And transracial adoptees see that. We see our differences, how our family ignores our race when it makes them more comfortable, and how they embrace our differences when it supports their narrative that love is the answer.

## TRANSRACIAL AND INTERNATIONAL ADOPTION

Intercountry adoption was uncommon until after World War II, when children who were orphaned were sent to the United States from Germany, Japan, and Greece. The Korean and Vietnam wars promoted an even larger surge of intercountry adoptions, often involving mixed-raced children. Before this, many countries did not have laws to protect the best interests of children being adopted abroad.[17]

Arguments against transracial and international adoption focus on forced global migration and the exploitation of poor countries. Since adoption is advantageous for white, middle-class infertile couples, some couples can forget the injustices that face poor women of color and poor white women. One of the first groups to argue against transracial adoption was Black social workers in the 1970s; they believed that transracial adoption threatens the personal development of Black children's identities and thought that white parents would be ill-prepared to help Black children against racism. Their claims are supported by the mixed results of the few studies that have been done on identity and development.[18] Other arguments focus on ethics, abuse in orphanages, fraud, and kidnapping. Some countries even started believing that intercountry adoption should be avoided and that the solution was to care for children within their birth country instead of adopting children out. Still others argue that international adoption violates human rights because it deprives children of their heritage birthright.[19] In countries like Australia and New Zealand, the transracial adoption of Aboriginal and Maori children is viewed by many as cultural genocide. In Switzerland, the adoption of Roma children is seen as similarly problematic.[20]

Despite the arguments, international adoptions are still very much in play. Often adopting from a poor country of origin is seen as easier than adopting children, especially Black children, from the foster care system.[21] Congress passed the Multiethnic Placement Act (MEPA) in 1994 and removed race from consideration for adoptive placements.[22] This made it easier for white, middle-class adoptive parents to adopt children of other races since the law did not form any federal guidelines; it left requirements up to adoption agencies to provide racial and cultural education. The problem with this is that the requirements that adoptive parents fulfill (i.e., racial competency, home studies, income, etc.) vary from each agency and state; some states still only require potential adoptive parents to fill out a questionnaire concerning their attitudes toward race and some require actual classes. Despite how it claims to increase the number of foster and adoptive families, MEPA does not mandate federal or even state funding to increase the outreach efforts to families of color.[23]

MEPA made colorblind placement legally mandatory in the US, except for Native American children who were subject to the Indian Child Welfare Act (ICWA). This federal law that governs the out-of-home placement of American Indian children passed in 1978 to protect Native American families from a biased welfare system. Prior to passage, Native Americans were three times more likely to be forcibly removed from their families of origin than non-Native children, and they were coerced into abusive boarding schools that stripped them of their customs, culture, and language. For example, at these boarding schools, their long hair was often cut into bowl cuts, their traditional clothing was taken away and replaced with uniforms, and they were punished for speaking their Native language. Between approximately 1860 and 1978 there were over 350 government-funded, often church-run boarding schools in the US; during this same time frame, the United States broke treaties and policies and started taking more tribal lands.[24]

Before the ICWA passed, about 75 percent of Native families living on reservations lost at least one child to the American foster care system. A statement by tribal Chief Calvin Isaac succinctly sums up the issue, "Many of the individuals who decide the fate of our children are, at best, ignorant of our cultural values and, at worst, have contempt for the Indian way and convinced that removal, usually to a non-Indian household or institution can only benefit an Indian child."[25]

Despite its implementation concerns, the ICWA has been labeled the gold standard of adoption laws by over eighteen child advocacy organizations.[26] It is important to note that even though ICWA emphasizes how important culture, community, and elders are, the law is not based on race but rather citizenship or membership in a federally recognized tribe. Despite the protection the ICWA afforded, white families have filed challenges over the years in order to adopt Native children, including some that had Native relatives who were seeking custody.[27] So while the ICWA offers some great protections, there are still loopholes, and if we compare the laws and protocols enacted domestically versus internationally, there are some significant differences in each.

The Hague Convention on the Protection of Children and Cooperation in Respect of Intercountry Adoption (shortened to the Hague Adoption Convention) mandates that countries protect the child's best interests. It aims to prevent the sale of, abduction of, or trafficking of children. According to the Hague Adoption Convention, intercountry adoption should be considered as a last option when a child has been deemed eligible for adoption; first, due consideration by the orphanage/agency needs to be given to finding an adoption placement in the child's country of origin.[28] Despite the Hague Adoption Convention's mandate, international adoption is seen as a first option by people wanting to adopt, often because adoptive parents' preferences are met more easily and with shortened wait times.[29]

Because adopting multiracial and biracial children became preferred when white babies weren't available for adoption in the 1950s, adoption agencies began bending the social norms of racial categorization of adoptees, particularly Black adoptees, to avoid the "one-drop rule" in favor of labeling infants with both Black and white heritage as multiracial. By including "white" or "multiracial" when labeling children up for adoption, adoption agencies have increased the adoptability of children considered as multiracial since research of pre-adoptive decisions has revealed a preference of "part-white" children among white adoptive couples.[30] This means white couples prefer and are more accepting of adopting multiracial and biracial children the closer they are to their perceived idea of whiteness.

Adoptive parents prefer adopting multiracial children because they believe they will have more in common with them and because they feel more legitimate by sharing racial ties with their adopted children. They also often feel less guilt for taking the children away from their community of origin and that mixed-race children will be less visibly different and "easier to explain" to relatives, friends, and neighbors.[31]

Although we know race is a social construct, in the United States, racial identity, especially the ideas of Black and white, is very important. Data from websites such as AdoptionNetwork .com and ParentProfile.com also show that adoptive parents strongly prefer Asian and Latinx children compared to Black children. In 2004, in an open directory project, ninety-six private agencies were analyzed in detail by looking at the drop-down menu options that pictured two and three-tiered adoption programs. In the menu, adoption agencies placed children depending on their ethnic/racial makeup, and often the way they choose to label Latinx and Asian infants in proximity to whiteness suggests social mobility to a place of being honorary white.[32]

The private agencies' programs separated children into different categories based on their race, many of which were labeled Traditional, Domestic, and Caucasian. The project found that the agencies carefully constructed each category to sort out which children could be classified as honorary members of the dominant society instead of applying a typical structure of Black, Asian, Indigenous, and so on. Many sites separated the categories further into Minority, African American/Biracial, Transracial, Diversity, and even Challenging. These agencies never included Latinx and Asian children in minority or diversity programs; only children of African American descent were. Often if the child was half white, they were placed in the Traditional tier, which meant adoptive parents were subjected to a different price range, wait time, marital requirements, familial structure, and age limits.[33] Data that illustrate the breakdown of categories, prices, and requirements for adoption are significant, but particularly so to me as an adoptee because they show how much race plays a factor in many adoption decisions. I find it interesting that Latinx and Asians are seen as "honorary white people."

In public, transracial adoptees are subjected to endless questions about racial ties to their adoptive family that require them to defend their own origin story. Since adoptees are more likely to be raised in primarily white neighborhoods, our parents' physical differences are often more evident. Questions like, "Where are you from?" or "Is that your real mom?" are often pressed upon us despite how complicated the answers may be.

Reports also show that adoptees, particularly Black adoptees, are more likely to be uncomfortable with their appearance and their social interactions with Black peers, especially during adolescence. One adoptee named Justine said that she felt nervous and feared her peers would say that she was not really Black enough, and that others would feel like she was a traitor.[34]

When you grow up surrounded by people of a different race, without a solid foundation of mirrors of people who look like you, it can be easy to become self-conscious—to desire the attributes of family and friends that you are constantly surrounded by. Transracial adoptees can struggle with developing a positive identity, which can make developing strong self-esteem difficult. It is also common for multiracial individuals to feel an "otherness" similar to transracial adoptees because they have different experiences than those who were raised in a single-race family.[35]

Despite all of this, many adoptive parents prefer to label their children as biracial versus Black but often do not socialize their adopted children to be bicultural, thus neglecting to pay significant attention to their child's Blackness.[36]

What stood out to me, is that despite the categorization that goes on, birth mothers of Black, Brown, and mixed-race babies often think that their children would have better lives outside of the racialized climate here in America; this is why babies are still being adopted to countries like Italy, Canada, the Netherlands, and Germany. Susan, a white American mother who adopted a multiracial child, said in an interview for CNN, that "there's too much prejudice over here. The white people are going to hate him because he is half Black, and the majority of Black people are going to hate on him because he's half white."[37]

Susan is not alone. Many birth parents who choose to place children via international adoption out of the United States believe that they will not experience as much discrimination in other countries like the Netherlands. Others have personal experiences within the foster care system that make them fear similar abuses for their children if they are left in the system, and so they also choose a couple not in the US. In 2010, the US State Department counted only forty-three children who were adopted overseas, but the Netherlands, Germany, and Switzerland combined reported around 205 children total who were adopted from the United States.[38]

When most adoptees, and even birth mothers, learn more about these facts on transracial and international adoption, they are left with some of the following questions.

*Isn't America supposed to be the place where people come for a "better life?"*

*If adoption is all about love, and color doesn't matter . . . why is there a price tag on us?*

*Why do some adoption agencies have lower fees to adopt a Black, Brown, or mixed-race baby?*

*Why do some birth mothers think that their children would have a better life in countries other than America?*

Adoptive families often say that they want to give a child a safe and loving home and often emphasize their pure intentions, but at the end of the day, the adoption industry is a business. But although agencies put price tags on babies and children, adoptive parents have the power to put pressure on the industry to have more ethical practices.

## FOSTER CARE

The foster care system was originally created in the 1930s to provide care for homeless and neglected children during the Great Depression. In the 1980s, it evolved into a social service aimed at healing youth with emotional, psychological, and behavioral issues, typically caused by abuse they experienced. The number of Black and Native American children in foster care is double that of their representation in the general child population. Ethnic minorities are more likely to be represented in foster care due to the disparate treatment that minorities face. Black children are more likely than any other ethnic group to be referred to protective services and have allegations of abuse substantiated.[39]

Black children are also less likely to be reunified with their birth families and more likely to experience longer stays in foster care, which has become a large reason why more Black children than white children are awaiting adoption. Compared to other children, studies have discovered that Hispanic children are more likely to remain in out-of-home placements for longer periods, are more likely to receive fewer mental health services, and are also less likely than white children to be adopted out of foster care.[40]

Most prospective adoptive parents tend to be well-educated, affluent white Americans. In certain states, structural barriers prevent more racially diverse prospective parents from adopting including marriage requirements, policies against couples who are LGBTQ+, and cultural biases by public adoption agencies that are less likely to approve Black applicants. Potential adoptive parents also show a preference for same-race placements and the 25 to 35 percent of prospective parents who are open to adopting children of a different race show a higher preference for younger children. This is one reason why MEPA received support to help place children who are likely to age out of foster care in adoptive homes since many studies have shown the benefits of placing a child for adoption are significant. When a child is adopted, benefits include having a stronger sense of belonging, being more resilient, and having better financial outcomes like being more highly educated and more financially well-off.[41]

Despite this, some child welfare professionals adamantly argue against placing children of color in foster care with white adoptive parents. This is largely due to a deficit in the ethnic identity development of transracial adoptees in white families. In fact, transracial adoptees experience a more significant drop in ethnic identity levels than children placed with parents of the same race.[42] (We discussed the importance of ethnic identity in Chapter 2.)

It is a pressing concern, in general, that children of color in the child welfare system face more disparities than their white counterparts, are less likely to be reunified with their birth family, are less likely to be matched with a permanent family, and are more likely to be placed in care settings.[43] The National Council on Crime and Delinquency has also found that girls, especially girls of color, in the foster care system have a higher recidivism rate, meaning that they are more likely to reenter the juvenile justice system than girls who have never had contact with the welfare system.[44] So when children of color are less likely to be placed in a permanent home, it can increase their risks when their time in the welfare system is prolonged.

It is essential to sit with the history of the foster care system and the adoption industry before you move forward in the adoption process. Some questions I encourage you to think about are these:

- How can you help children without benefitting from a corrupt system built on systemic racism?

- Do you feel like fostering and adoption are a type of white saviorism? Why or why not?

- Do you think there are ways to encourage family preservation?

- Do you feel equipped to raise a child of color?

- How do you think a parent of color parents differently than you do as a white person?

- What benefits are there to children of color being raised by other people of color?

- What do you bring to the table that they can't?

## REPRODUCTIVE HEALTH

When we talk about adoption, it is important to look at data that has affected the number of adoptions occurring in the United States. When abortions in the United States were legalized, the number of adoptions decreased significantly.[45] Before 1973 about 9 percent of never-married women chose adoption; by the mid-1980s, it dropped to 2 percent; and by 2002, the number of women who chose adoption was less than 1 percent.[46] A study in 2016 found that most women who are denied abortions choose to parent their child, and the women who do choose adoption are less likely to be employed but more likely to finish high school.[47] These statistics are significant when you consider the number of women who now have the power to choose whether to abort, put their baby up for adoption, or parent, since the stigma of unwed mothers has reduced.

And yet, the pressure by others in society is still high as political right-wing groups continue to promote pro-life stances and adoption despite data that indicate women would rather parent their own children than choose adoption. If the data supports this, it is frustrating to me and many adoptees that single mothers lack support from our government, when so much money is spent advertising against Planned Parenthood and on bulletin boards that promote choosing adoption over funding programs that help these women in crisis parent.

Google Ads that pop up in my browser if I look up the terms *adoption, birth family, young mom,* and more are another persistent example of how money is spent on advertising. Just recently, an ad popped up that said, "Pregnant and Need Money? Choose Adoption." Another that said "Couple Hoping to Adopt" popped up on Google as I was searching for resources for birth moms. As an adoptee, seeing how predatory agencies can be toward expectant parents made me feel disgusted and frustrated; I quickly took a screenshot to share with the adoption community on my Instagram page @adoptee_thoughts.[48] The idea that adoption agencies and adoptive parents seem to be infallible is very troubling to me, and I needed to speak with others who understood the pain I felt when reading those ads. What felt most problematic to me was that my Instagram post received more than twenty comments containing other adoptees' experiences, and many others added that hashtags on social media by prospective adoptive parents are incredibly disappointing and triggering. No one should target women who are #pregnantandafraid with an #unplannedpregnancy and think that it's ethical to try to influence them so that they can adopt their baby.

More pro-adoption advertising examples include a 2013 national ad campaign by Heroic Media and an ad that Bethany

Christian Services aired that featured a pregnant woman explaining why she was choosing adoption. Bill Blacquiere, then CEO of Bethany, told the Catholic News Agency that the commercial was aired in the hope of connecting women with adoption resources. Organizers later said that hundreds of women contacted Bethany Christian Services and that the ad was intended to show adoption as a positive solution and an alternative for a birth mother, and the media director of the commercial used phrases such as "gift of love and hope" and "life-changing blessing."[49] Other examples of adoption advertising include the Google and Facebook ads that advertise adoption as the best option and showcase a beautiful, adoptive couple looking to adopt. Couples often spend thousands of dollars in advertising fees to "save" a child, rather than putting that money toward funding for programs that would help the family stay together or even fostering older children in foster care.

It's important to note that thirty-three states have laws that regulate the use of advertising in adoptive placement to protect the interests of all parties, particularly the children, but only five states prohibit advertising to find a child to adopt or rehome. Alabama and Kentucky prohibit any advertising related to adoption by any entity, North Dakota prohibits advertisement by hospitals providing maternity care, in Virginia no agency or person can advertise to perform any adoption-related activity prohibited by state law, and Utah prohibits advertising by doctors, attorneys, or unlicensed persons unless it's stated in the ad. Eleven states limit advertising to only state social services or licensed agencies. Additionally, other states allow *intermediaries* or *adoption facilitators* that help match a birth parent with a prospective adoptive parent; however, forty-three states have laws that regulate the use of intermediaries in order to try and prevent profit from child placement.[50]

When we think about advertising and the use of intermediaries, it is important to consider who is benefiting the most, especially after you factor in the power dynamic in the adoption community. After all, adoptive parents hold all of the power once the birth parents sign the adoption papers. When adoptive parents have the power to raise funds and the community support behind them to adopt, expectant moms can feel even more pressure to place their children for adoption. Is it really fair to target vulnerable women in need of help with such advertising and practices that offer help as long as they consider adoption? To me, as an adoptee, this seems rather predatory and unethical.

For example, in a recent post on Twitter, a woman asks for advice on whether she should take her friend to get an abortion even though she personally is pro-life.[51] As of July of 2020, there were over 8,000 comments on this post before the original was deleted; most either told her not to support her friend or to push her friend to consider adoption. One particular comment said, "I am an adoptive parent, it would so warm my heart if you could talk yr [your] friend into giving up the child to a couple who so desperately wants a family." And then it continues . . . "So many couples 'desperately' want a child BUT feel that there is no possibility of getting to that point. So many pregnant women who feel desperate & abort . . ."[52] Another comment said, "As someone who suffers from infertility and who has had three miscarriages, I still feel if it's not used as a form of birth control, it's the women's choice. With that being said, I'd be happy to adopt her baby if she would choose that route instead."[53]

In a post on *Slate*'s parenting advice column, a reader, self-titled "Auntie's Baby, Maybe," wrote in a letter titled "I Don't Think My Niece Is Ready for a Baby. Should I Take the Child?"[54] In the letter the reader shares how her niece is only twenty-one, currently unemployed, has no permanent address, and is without health insurance due to her lack of motivation to sign forms on time. Auntie's Baby, Maybe adds that she and her partner of eight years have a spare bedroom and that she feels better prepared than her niece because she has been around babies her whole life. Even though, as she mentions, her niece wants the baby, the letter writer wants advice on what to do. She has an unfounded belief that the baby will experience neglect.

Thankfully, the *Slate* columnist suggested that the aunt think things over, offer her niece a safe place to live, and even offer child care while she gets on her feet. To see that there are people out there whose first instinct is to offer to take a woman's baby rather than to support her in her time of need is incredibly frustrating. The fact that this woman was also a biological family member to the expectant mother and an adoptee herself was also problematic. However, I was not very surprised by her behavior since Americans put such an emphasis on *individualism*, the idea that freedom of thought and action for each person is the most important quality of a society, rather than a shared effort and responsibility.[55]

Let's get one thing straight. Adoption is an alternative to parenting, not pregnancy.

When people, especially other women, pressure expectant parents to choose to place their child for adoption, perhaps it is due to the strong correlation between the availability of abortions and the number of infants up for adoption. Some people may assume that adoption is the best option for women in need, but it is also important to note that pregnancies can have complications that threaten the mother's health along the way. I personally had cholestasis of pregnancy, preterm labor, and other issues, including an emergency surgery at twenty-one weeks that put not only my health but my baby's in jeopardy.

I understand that infertility is a hard pill to swallow for any person with a female reproductive system, but it is never okay to put pressure on another pregnant person because they are pregnant and do not want to continue the pregnancy. The reasons a person chooses to terminate a pregnancy are honestly only important for that person and their doctor.

It's also important to note that the comments made by women who promote adoption first focus on the infertile women who want babies rather than the struggling pregnant woman who should have been given help in her time of need. Even if you do not support abortion for religious or other reasons, you can *support* pregnant people instead of trying to take advantage of their situation like those in the comments I mentioned earlier.

As an adoptee, I find it sickening when people suggest that unwed and low-income parents "simply" give up their children for adoption and offer to take care of the child instead of offering a helping hand to the parents. For example, by supporting family planning services and comprehensive sexual education, you can help prevent unwanted pregnancies in the first place. You can donate money and time and promote educational programs for low-income/pregnant people—perhaps you can volunteer and support parenting classes for teen mothers, or low-income housing. Most importantly, offer a judgment-free ear for the pregnant person to lean on in the time of need. Be the village for that pregnant person.

## CHILD TRAFFICKING

*Child trafficking* is defined as the recruitment, transfer, harboring of, or receipt of a child for the purpose of sexual or labor exploitation or slavery.[56] *Illegal adoptions* are defined as those that result from abduction, sale, or trafficking in children, fraud, falsification of official documents, or coercion.[57] When you think about child trafficking and illegal adoption practices, you might think that they seem like a problem of the past, like the Baby Scoop Era or Operation Babylift (defined and discussed later in this chapter). Honestly, I wish that was the case; in fact, child trafficking is still happening.

## Marshall Islands Trafficking Scandal

Hearing stories like these can be frightening and disheartening, and you may even think that you could never be part of something like illegal adoptions. But unfortunately, some adoption agencies are also involved in shady practices that use ethical gray areas and adoptive parents' desire for a baby to cloud their judgment. In this section, I cover a brief history of human trafficking and adoption.

Paul Petersen, a United States Republican and former politician, plead guilty in June of 2020 to human smuggling and various other charges related to an illegal adoption scheme in three states, in which he took advantage of women from the Marshall Islands. Originally, Petersen was charged with illegally paying women to come to the United States to give their babies up for adoption. This lasted for about three years and resulted in about seventy adoption cases in Utah, Arizona, and Arkansas. The women who were brought to Utah had little prenatal care, and their passports were taken once they arrived in the United States. Petersen pleaded guilty in Utah to one count of communications fraud and three counts of human smuggling, which are all felonies.[58] In December of 2020, he was sentenced to seventy-four months in federal prison for his illegal adoption scam, that the judge called a "get-rich-quick scheme . . . hidden behind the shiny veneer of a humanitarian operation."[59]

Petersen, a dedicated member of the Church of Jesus Christ of Latter-day Saints, completed a mission trip in the Marshall Islands, where he learned the language and began facilitating adoptions. It seems like an odd coincidence that text messages and interviews found by *The Arizona Republic* showed that he placed children with Latter-day Saints families frequently despite the Church's officials saying that they did not sanction his conduct.[60] Many of the illicit adoptions followed a similar pattern. Petersen paid individuals to locate pregnant women interested in adoption, and then he would match them with adoptive families in the United States. He then paid each pregnant woman about $1,000 per month and promised them up to $10,000 to place their unborn child for adoption. He then charged each adoptive family $35,000, claiming to use part of the money for the birth mother's medical costs, which was not the case. Instead, it was found that he had signed the mothers up for Medicaid benefits in Arizona and claimed they were residents.[61]

## US Border Crisis

As of October of 2020, the government still had not found over 500 children who were separated from their parents during Trump's immigration crackdown at the United States and Mexican border. The ACLU stated that their efforts to reunite families have been hindered by incomplete government reports and difficult conditions in the children's native lands. Department of Homeland Security officials have said the government is working to reunite the children but have found that some parents do not want to claim their children because not claiming them allows the children to stay in the United States. Others hope to be reunited in the United States. Between July 2017 and June 2018, over 1,500 children were separated from their families, and by the time the district Judge Dana Sabraw issued a reunification order, many parents were unaccounted for. Advocates continue to try to reunite families, but often lawyers must rely on networking with nonprofit staff and human rights lawyers led by Justice in Motion, a group that is on the ground trying to track down families in El Salvador, Mexico, Honduras, and Guatemala. Such groups have had to pause their efforts due to the coronavirus.[62]

For a few years, families coming into the US through the Texas border seeking asylum have consistently run the risk of losing their children. In 2018, US officials said that over 200 remain ineligible for reunification or release. In addition, a major loophole in the system was found by the Associated Press that allowed state court judges (in Central America) to grant custody of migrant children to American families without notifying the child's parents, who are often deported hundreds of miles away. State courts often seal records in child custody cases, and the federal agencies involved in such immigration cases do not keep track of these records.[63]

Alexa was one such woman who was separated from her fifteen-month-old daughter and had to fight tooth and nail to get her back. Her daughter was placed in the United States foster care, run by the agency Bethany Christian Services, after they were separated at the border. This agency recently acknowledged that since the 1980s, some of the migrant children it was assigned were adopted by American families, despite the fact that foster families are not "allowed" to adopt migrant children.[64]

## The Baby Scoop Era

The *Baby Scoop Era* refers to the time between 1945 and 1971 when over 1.5 million unwed mothers were pressured into giving up their babies for adoption. During this time period, access to birth control and sex education were very limited and far behind where they are today; in some states, birth control was illegal for those who were unmarried. The girls and women who found themselves with unwanted pregnancies during this time period were pressured by social service agencies, their clergy, their family members, and society in general to give up their child for adoption. Adoption was seen as the only acceptable option; anything else lead to shame for the unwed mother and entire family, and often led to ostracization. During this time, these women were told to stay quiet, move on, and forget what happened.[65]

Barb Larson was one such mother who was pressured into a forced adoption of her son. When she became pregnant, she was just a sophomore in high school who knew very little about sex and had very Catholic parents. After her parents discovered she was pregnant, they set up a plan, like hundreds of other parents had during that time. Barb was sent to another city, was unable to speak about her pregnancy, and had her baby in secret. Specifically, Barb was sent to stay with relatives in Toledo where she spent her days at the Florence Crittenton home for unwed mothers. Barb was not allowed to see her son after giving birth and was forced to sign the adoption papers without being given any other option.[66]

## Operation Babylift

*Operation Babylift* occurred in 1975 at the end of the Vietnam War when President Ford directed funds from foreign aid to fly around 2,000 orphans from South Vietnam to the United States. Many of these orphans were under two years old and had to be carried onto the plane. Dennis Traynor, the pilot of the first of these flights had to crash land the cargo plane due to a malfunction that resulted in the death of 78 children and 50 adults. When the children eventually reached the United States, they were given new names, and since there was no passenger manifest, it has been difficult to trace the children.[67]

It has since been found that many of these children were not actually orphans; those who were fathered by American soldiers were thought to be in danger as the communists advanced in South Vietnam. At the time, Graham Martin, the American Ambassador in Vietnam, stated that the evacuation would help improve the American public opinion. President Ford used the opportunity to take advantage of the photos taken at the airport with airlifted children. Some saw this as an attempt to gain sympathy and approval for the war by showing the "saving" of orphans, but others felt that the orphans may not have needed saving at all and were perhaps lost and taken from their community and culture.[68] It was actually common practice at the time for poor families in Vietnam to place their children in orphanages if they could not care for them, but they still visited their children. Many children were adopted out of these orphanages, despite the lack of consent from their parents. Even though a case that expressed ethical concerns about Operation Babylift was brought to courts by Bay Area attorney Tom Miller, the case was dismissed, and the records were sealed.[69]

## Baby Factories

In Nigeria, illegal shelters that are involved in exploiting young girls who have given birth to children for illegal adoption and trafficking are referred to as the *baby factories*. The continued prevalence of baby factories in Nigeria is often due to the high rates of poverty in the country and the constant demand for infant children by childless couples around the world. Adoption rings can make a lucrative profit off of this supply and demand. In baby factories there are many cases of abuse of underaged girls who are used for child labor and are often forced to give birth to unwanted pregnancies; children born into these places can be used for child labor, as child soldiers, and even for prostitution. Young girls are often tricked into the factories by being promised help and support during their pregnancies. There have also been documented reports of young girls being kidnapped, impregnated, and held until they give birth.[70]

Nigeria is just one of several countries to engage in illegal and unethical practices so it is very important for prospective adoptive parents who are interested in adoption (particularly international adoption) to do their due diligence in making sure everything is legal and appropriate. Here are some questions to ask to help you steer clear of unethical agencies and orphanages.

**Red Flags Adoptive Parents Can Look For**

- How does the adoption agency talk about expectant (birth) parents? Are the agencies working to protect their rights?

- Does the agency call the pregnant parent a "birth" parent before the baby has been born?

- How does the agency interact with expectant parents? Read the section of their website aimed at expectant parents.

- How does the agency get in contact with birth parents?

- How does the agency handle the rights of birth fathers? Do they encourage mothers not to name the father?

- Does the agency support family preservation first?

- Does the agency encourage the expectant mom to spend time with her baby after giving birth even if adoption papers were signed?

- Are the agency's licensing requirements up to date?

- Where is your money going? Most agencies offer a breakdown of fees. Will your agency answer any questions you have?

- Does the agency offer shorter wait times for higher fees? Do they participate in race-based pricing?

- Do you feel pressure from the agency to act now?

- What does the agency do if the birth parent decides against adoption and chooses to parent? Do they provide the pregnant person with resources?

- Does the agency pressure expectant parents to sign consent for adoption prior to giving birth in order to receive resources?

- Does the agency have pregnancy and post-placement counseling for expectant parents?

- Does the agency offer long-term support for all adoption triad members?

*NOTE* *If adoption agencies are unable to answer any of these questions, I urge you to step back, pause, and do more research before continuing. No one can guarantee you a baby. Adoptions fall through sometimes, whether the person chooses to parent, loses the baby, or even chooses a different family. If an adoption agency offers a quick adoption or a guaranteed adoption, these are some serious red flags that are telling you to stop and begin looking for a more ethical agency. Please do not ignore these signs.*

## LACK OF CITIZENSHIP

When children are adopted by American parents and raised in America, you would think that would automatically give them citizenship in the United States. Unfortunately, it is not that simple.

Thousands of adoptees are discovering that they aren't US citizens, even after decades of living here with American parents. Adoptees are learning that, due to their adoptive parents', agencies', or lawyers' failure to file the correct paperwork, they do not have citizenship, even if the parents thought they had done everything correctly. Often, these children and their parents may not even realize that there is a problem until they try to travel internationally or undergo a secure background check.[71]

There are approximately 15,000 to 18,000 adults who were adopted by United States citizens who do not have citizenship, but the exact number is unclear because the government doesn't keep track. Thankfully, Congress passed the Child Citizenship Act of 2000, which gives automatic citizenship to international adoptees. The one problem is that the child must have been under the age of eighteen as of February 27, 2001, in order to receive citizenship.[72] Because there is no law that grants citizenship to international adoptees of every age, many adoptees fear separation from their families and, often, the only home they have ever known. In fact, until the 2000s, children adopted internationally needed to be naturalized to receive citizenship. Without the citizenship, adoptees in this situation are left stumbling to apply for visas and green cards. Some are denied, and can be deported to their birth countries where they struggle immensely without knowing the culture and language, and without connections to known family.[73] Deported adoptees also face some difficulty finding work and housing. Their experience is made even more difficult by language barriers, lack of transportation, and lack of connections within the country. In episode 6 of the *Adoptee Thoughts* podcast, Anissa Druesedow, an international adoptee originally from Jamaica, shared her struggle to find a family to care for her daughter while she tried to find her footing in her birth country after being deported. Anissa was adopted into a military family as a little girl and faced many struggles throughout her life. She was diagnosed with cancer as a teen and had to undergo a leg amputation to save her life.[74] When Anissa grew up, she found herself pressured into marrying a man who soon became abusive. She was able to escape the abuse with her daughter but then struggled without the support of a husband or her adoptive family. While struggling to make ends meet as a single mom and working long hours, she was approached by a friend to return items without a receipt. Months later she was arrested and convicted of grand larceny. Her public defender convinced her to plead guilty in order to get out of jail quicker on work release than she would if she fought the charges.

*I got an Order of deportation sent to me via the mail at Albion, Women's Correctional Facility . . . So, I call my mom, and I'm like, Mom, what is happening? I have an order of deportation. What is going on? And you know, she's like, well, if you hadn't gotten in trouble, none of this would be happening.*[75]

She was told by her public defender that she should receive a maximum sentence of three months and be back with her daughter quickly. But then she received an unexpected visit from ICE who told her that her parents never finalized her adoption. Without the support of her adoptive parents, she was soon deported. As a person with a disability, she had difficulty trying to find work and was separated by thousands of miles from her child.

Many adoptees like Anissa do not realize that they do not have citizenship until they apply for a passport, commit a crime (no matter how small), go through a security background check, or try to vote thinking that they have the right to do so. Because they've paid taxes and used a social security card for years, many international adoptees do not realize that their citizenship is in question until these instances occur and the government finally digs and finds that the proper paperwork was never filed, lawyers were misinformed, or adoptive parents simply took too long to fill out paperwork.[76]

Ultimately, Anissa was let down by her adoptive parents who failed to file the proper paperwork to ensure her citizenship. Her story is just one of the thousands. Each one illustrates the need for the government to pass the Adoptee Citizenship Act to prevent adoptees from being torn away from their adoptive family, their friends, and their children after they have already had to deal with the trauma of being separated from their first families.

In 2015 and 2018, the Adoptee Citizenship Act proposed to Congress would have granted automatic citizenship to adult adoptees, but it never made it out of committee. Advocacy groups, such as the Adoptee Rights Campaign and Adoptees for Justice, are still advocating for citizenship for all foreign-born American adoptees.[77] It is essential for laws like the Adoptee Citizenship Act to pass so all international adoptees can have access to the same rights as biological children.

In the meantime, there are a few easy ways to help. First call or write to your congressional members and let them know you support the Adoptee Citizenship Act and citizenship for all adoptees. Next, donate to causes like the Adoptee Defense Fund to help adoptees without citizenship pay legal fees. Then meet with your congressional representatives to build support for the bill; it is essential to create a rapport with representatives and senators. Groups like Adoptees for Justice can walk you through how to do this on their website. Finally, you can always sign petitions in order to demonstrate support for the Adoptee Citizenship Act.

## THE BUSINESS OF ADOPTION

*Consumerism* is the idea that customer spending is the key driver of the economy. Encouraging consumers, or in this case, adoptive parents, is the goal. Consumerism is prominently displayed in the adoption industry as prospective parents discuss the selection process and why they are choosing certain countries over others to adopt from.[78] When coming to the decision to adopt, certain factors weigh heavily on adoptive parents. Should they choose an open versus closed adoption? Domestic versus international? The options available for adoption in the twenty-first century are endless, but at the end of the day, a certain factor tends to give many pause—the cost.

Adoption is a very profitable business for adoption agencies. In 2004, in Florida, adoption revenues reached $1.44 billion, with a projected annual growth of 11.5 percent.[79] And, it doesn't come as a surprise to many that adoption fees add up quickly. The US Department of Health and Human Services says that adopting through an agency in a domestic adoption can cost between $25,000 and $50,000. These costs usually cover legal fees, medical and living expenses for the expectant mom, travel costs, and a home study. Home studies are required for both international and domestic adoptions from private or foster care in the United States. The study entails criminal background checks, financial checks, and even checks on the personal relationships of each prospective parent.[80]

Independent adoptions, according to the Child Welfare Information Gateway, can occur when an expectant mother and adoptive parents find each other without the help of an agency and can range from $15,000 to $40,000. Independent adoptions are similar to selling a house on your own: you have to figure out where to advertise to appeal to pregnant mothers and learn how to vet pregnant moms. Then you'll need to add in all the usual costs of the home study, medical expenses, and legal fees.[81]

Meanwhile, adopting from foster care is essentially free because states often reimburse adoptive parents for the adoption fees. Still, since reunification, not adoption, is the foster care system's main goal—many potential adoptive parents would rather go another route. Although there are thousands of children whose parents terminated their parental rights in the foster care system and who are looking for adoptive families, those children are often older.

Next is international adoption, where, according to the Child Welfare Information Gateway, adoptive parents can expect to pay between $20,000 and $50,000.[82] In addition to the typical costs, multiple flights to and from the country of origin and other hotel and travel costs add up. Those undeterred by the potential costs of adoption can raise the funds by turning to employer benefits, tax credits, or loans, by asking for help from family or friends, and by fundraising. Prospective parents can also apply for *adoption grants*, financially risk-free options typically awarded by nonprofit organizations that can help adoptive families reach their financial goals. A quick Google search for grants will give you dozens of options to apply for that are very commonly used in the adoption community.

The adoption industry has struggled with ethical issues over the years as well as trafficking, as discussed earlier in this chapter; however, in 1993, sixty-six countries gathered together to create the Convention on Protection of Children and Co-Operation in Respect to Intercountry Adoption during a Hague Conference on Private International Law.[83]

When you think about the adoption of a child, what comes to mind? I know that I would expect a complicated array of forms, home studies, and recommendation letters from friends, family, and employees. But what I didn't expect was that social workers have little leeway in whose applications they are allowed to turn down, even if they have doubts that the couple is fit to adopt. Some social workers even say that they often prefer that prospective clients come to the realization that they shouldn't adopt by themselves, partly to protect themselves from more pain after experiencing losses via miscarriage. An example from the book *Selling Transracial Adoption* that stands out to me was when an adoptive parent called to ask if "adopting an African child would signal to her white children that it was acceptable to marry a Black person."[84]

The fact that social workers seemed pressured to approve families because they fear being labeled difficult to work with reminds me of the quotas I had to meet when I worked in sales. When you have a customer-is-always-right, or in this case, let-the-customer-decide-for-themselves mentality, it doesn't seem like the system is actually working to protect vulnerable children and birth parents from choosing adoptive parents who aren't ready for the challenges adoption may bring.

The unfortunate truth is that the adoption industry isn't focused on making education a requirement. When adoption social workers hope to push for education, without a way to make it required, it seems wholly irresponsible for them to approve adoptive parents when they, the professionals, have doubts. Adoptive parents adopting internationally from countries that have signed the Hague treaty are required to complete ten hours of education and training; but only thirteen states in the United States require this.[85] Instead, agencies focus on fees, marketing to adoptive families, and paying for ads to entice birth mothers to choose adoption in order to make sure they have enough babies available to feed the constant demand for infants.

When adoption is set up in a way in which agencies and private attorneys make thousands of dollars off of adoption fees and services, it makes sense to look at adoption as a business. And like every business structure, there is a supply and demand. Supply is defined by how much of something you have, and demand is how much of something people want. In adoption, the supply and demand refer to the number of children available for adoption and how much parents are willing to pay.[86] When there is an increase in the demand for children due to infertility rates, among other things, adoption agencies feel free to increase prices and push for more adoptions to feed their business. And while adoption is a for-profit business, can we really trust that agencies are trying to keep families together? Or is it more likely that they will do what benefits their business most?

As an adoptee, it is hard not to think about the impact of this side of adoption when a common deciding factor for adoptive parents is cost. It makes me feel like a prized possession that my parents saved up to purchase and this is a stark reminder that adoption is not just about love. Adoptive parents yearn for a certain type of product (or, in this case, baby), which is a driving factor that impacts the adoption industry's business structure. The fact that older children in foster care are less desirable impacts the cost of infants and makes agencies put out frequent ads to get the attention of pregnant women to make sure they are keeping up with the demand. And when the supply for young infants is not meeting the demand of adoptive parents, agencies can hike up prices to increase profits. If adoptions were just about providing homes for children in need, they would be free or low cost like most foster-to-adopt situations. In fact, most adoptions from foster care are funded by the state, and in those cases, they are often low cost or no fee.[87]

# 4

## INFLUENCERS, SOCIAL MEDIA ETIQUETTE, THE CHURCH, AND THE FALLACY OF GIVING ADOPTED CHILDREN A BETTER LIFE

*L*ife is subjective.

This is a concept that most people learn early on. But when it comes to adoption, we all need to remember that when you adopt a child, you are not giving that child a "better" life. You are giving them a *different* life. *Better* is also a subjective concept and many confuse being financially stable or having lots of material things with being in a better situation.

You can have a great life with a family that you love even if you do not have half the opportunities or money that others have. We, as a society, forget the often-immediate disadvantages that mothers of color face when parenting. One telling example of this is Black women's higher mortality rate when giving birth.[1]

Many people automatically assume an adopted child is beyond lucky, and tell them so, and forget that the adoptive parents are gaining a child that another family lost. And they are gaining a child who lost their original family.

Remember, adoption isn't better; it's different.

Adoption can be just as problematic for a child, or even more so, than having a single parent who has financial struggles or is unstable. Sometimes unstable or unprepared adoptive families can lead to a child being rehomed if adoptive parents are not satisfied with the transaction, particularly when international adoption agencies make promises to adoptive families about a child's physical and mental health. *Rehoming* in adoption is the unregulated custody transfer of a child to another family without the welfare system's involvement. Families will typically use online groups or even forums to rehome children without any government oversight or background or criminal checks of the child's new family. According to the Department of Health and Human Services, children who are rehomed are at a greater risk for abuse, neglect, or exploitation.[2]

One rehoming case in particular that sticks out for me is that of the infamous family YouTuber Myka Stauffer and her adopted son Huxley. She and her husband created a profitable YouTube channel with over 700,000 fans that took off in 2014 after she shared their journey to adopt Huxley; then she announced that they were placing him in a new home that could better address his medical needs.[3] This case gained a lot of media attention due to the celebrity of Huxley's adoptive parents, but what is important to learn from it is that the rehoming of adopted children is not that uncommon. In the United States, between 1 and 5 percent of adoptions are dissolved like the Stauffers'. On top of that, between 10 and 25 percent of adoptions are *disrupted*, which means that the adoption ends before it becomes legally finalized.[4]

## PREYING ON PREGNANT MOTHERS ON THE INTERNET

In the United States, it has become common for women to post on social media about their families' desire to adopt and even start searching online for potential birth mothers. Americans are driven to seek out private adoptions online since international adoptions have become more regulated by countries like China, Guatemala, and Russia. Since there are fewer babies to adopt internationally through traditional methods, such as adoption agencies, the environment has become very competitive for adoptive parents . . . which leads to women seeking out mothers online.

American families often hold photo shoots and pose for "bump" shots with letterboards cleverly posed over barren stomachs that they then share in their communities or online in hopes of connecting with pregnant people. "Hoping to Adopt" or "No Bump, Still Pumped," are some of the phrases that are perfectly placed. The families use the resulting images, with the smiling faces and clever hashtags, to advertise that they are looking for pregnant women who want to place their children for adoption. Ads like these are often placed with a plea for friends, family, and complete strangers to share far and wide; they also often urge expectant mothers considering adoption to contact them.

An example of this is the account of Jamie Dorn, an English teacher, who, in June of 2018, decided to make an Instagram account to try to convince a pregnant stranger that her family was a good match to adopt her baby. Jamie and her husband created an account @JamieAndBrianAdopt (that no longer exists) and then posted every day like their friends in the adoption community suggested. They used hashtags like #hopetoadopt and #adoptionrocks to get as much attention on their profile as possible; their posts were full of pictures of fishing and celebrating the Fourth of July. It took only six weeks of this for them to receive an email from a pregnant woman in her first trimester; just seven months later, they adopted her baby. Jamie even said, "Social media is amazing in this sense; we completed our family because of it."[5]

Some families spend hundreds of dollars on Google ads to help their profiles pop up for mothers considering adoption. Others hire adoption advertising businesses, like First Steps Advertising for Adoption, to handle their profile books and social media campaigns.[6] But while prospective parents are spending all this money on advertising, birth mothers are struggling to make it from day-to-day with little support from family, friends, and society.

When it comes to deciding to place a child for adoption, financial needs are arguably the number one consideration. From a lack of familial support, to homelessness, to, sometimes, addiction, myriad nuanced reasons go into a mother's decision to place a child for adoption.[7] But in this day and age, with adoption ads all over social media, I believe it is too easy for expectant mothers to be forced to compare themselves to what others say they can provide. The weight of motherhood has become heavier with the rise of social media, where all mothers can easily view one another with one click; think of this compared to the past, when mothers could only compare themselves to family, friends they knew personally, and television.

I cannot quite imagine the weight of the decision to place a child for adoption. After hearing more of my birth mom's story, I understand how vulnerable she was. I was my birth mother's fourth biological child and the third to be placed for adoption. Abuse played a role in why she was on her own without her extended family's support; she was fired from her job when her boss discovered she was pregnant. She had to sell flowers on the street to make it through each day. My birth mother fought hard to keep her children, but eventually, homelessness and lack of funds were the deciding factors for her. She wanted to make sure that her daughters had a stable environment, and, ultimately, opportunities that she could not provide due to her circumstances.

However, the picture-perfect, white picket fences portrayed in filtered images of couples looking for babies is a risky place for a birth mother to start analyzing the family she may place her child with. Instagram and Facebook can cause so many problems for birth moms; for instance, these moms may end up comparing themselves to the images that are portrayed, even though such images are often an unreliable indicator of an adoptive parent's true character and daily life. Information about the potential adoptive family presented in such platforms can be misleading, although their skewed presentation can fool anyone into thinking that the family is perfect and that they are more deserving because they own giant letterboards, matching outfits, and big houses. These social media posts are why I and many other adoptees I know are adamantly against adoption advertising; they highlight its predatory and ethically questionable tactics.

So again, the internet is not a reliable place for finding people to adopt your baby.

A heartbreaking story of what can happen if a birth mom trusts such advertising is the story involving Jennifer Talbot, an American who was arrested in the Philippines for trying to smuggle a six-day-old baby boy past immigration officials. She claimed to be the baby's aunt but was soon charged with human trafficking, kidnapping, illegal detention, and child abuse. The baby's mother told the officials that she met Talbot online and discussed adoption, which is a story many other birth mothers can relate to.[8]

Talbot started off just like many other women hoping to adopt, posting ads on social media about hoping to adopt a child or a small sibling group. "We are looking to adopt. We have a huge home and even larger heart . . . If you or someone you know may be considering adoption, please let us help." In the ads DailyMail.com was able to retrieve, she claimed that her children went to private school, that her family went to church every Sunday, and she even included what she referred to as "candid" photos of her family. But anonymous sources close to the family shared that the family rarely went to church, and that Talbot was desperate for a baby. It wasn't long after these posts appeared that she was arrested by the Filipino authorities.[9]

When placing a child for adoption in the right home becomes a competition, when it is about who has the better pictures on Instagram and the cleverest caption, it becomes a competition that no one wins . . . especially the adopted child.

It has become all too easy for people to seek out pregnant women who are single, low-income, have multiple children, and do not have a stable home. As a woman with two biological children, I remember how difficult the changes a woman goes through during pregnancy are even without pressure from others to give up their baby for a "better life." At such a vulnerable point in our lives, it can be easier to believe promises from agencies of happy childhoods with perfect private schools and designer clothes; these make new moms susceptible to making choices they are not 100 percent comfortable with.

When women face unexpected pregnancies, and government support is not enough or is nonexistent, they can turn to the internet for help; when they do, they are often faced with the beautiful and often misleading picture-perfect answer of adoption. Meanwhile, programs aimed to help young women or mothers in need, like WIC or SNAP, often face budget cuts.[10]

The weight of toxic positivity surrounds the adoption community and often paints the picture of a happily-ever-after story when adoption is much more than that. The trauma that occurs when children are separated from birth families is long lasting and not portrayed in these heavily filtered Instagram pictures and captions. The fact that adoptees are four times more likely to attempt suicide is not discussed.[11] Social media falsely portrays adoption as a simple solution to global societal issues when, in reality, adoption is a Band-Aid for what happens when we fail to support those of us in need.

## UNDERCOVER REALITIES

Many adoptees scroll through adoptee support groups on Facebook or browse on Twitter to find support in our community, but often we are exposed to the harsh realities of adoptive parents baring their truth without considering the effects they may have on adopted persons or even birth mothers. For instance, they might post comparing adopted children with biological children, or criticizing an adoptee's sometimes challenging behavior, while using #adoptivefamily or other adoption-related tags, thus letting the world know more about the adoptee's personal history than they should.

Recently, in my support group for transracial adoptees and adoptive families, I stumbled across comments from a few white adoptive parents. One said that "my adopted child is happy she's adopted rather than aborted." Another made a similar comment on a thread on Twitter, perhaps with the best intentions. It is important to note that although the intention was to simply share your experience, in that effort, you also silence the voices of adoptees that are telling their truth . . . their *lived* experiences.

In the same adoption group, a parent asked for advice about the birth mother asking to have sleepovers with her child. The original poster was hesitant to allow it and stated that her husband does not like how open the adoption is and would prefer that it was closed. Some of the advice included empathetic comments that suggested immediately setting strong boundaries. Others were sympathetic to the birth mother and suggested the adoptive mother consider the birth mother's plea to "share." Still, most were very against the trajectory that the relationship seemed to be taking.

A few comments that stood out to me as an adoptee were the following:

> I'm sorry she is starting to overstep boundaries. She is not the Mother figure here, and unless you have an open adoption, she is getting to be any part of her life because you allow it. You should remind her of that . . . Sharing is where it would start. The more she gives, the more the birth Mom would ask for, and from there, you end up with a lot of drama. She already gets more than she should.[12]

> She is YOUR daughter. There is no "shared parenting" unless it's with your partner.[13]

I wish I could say that it was surprising to me that so many adoptive parents implied that it wasn't a wise choice and outright stated that the adoptive mother should shut down the birth mom's request to connect with her daughter. It was also hard to miss the overwhelming need by adoptive parents responding to the post to state that the child was *hers* (i.e., the adoptive mom's), and therefore that her feelings and needs should be prioritized. These reactions are, unfortunately, very familiar, despite the common knowledge that open adoptions can be very beneficial for the child. It seems as if adoptive parents need to do what's easiest for them despite what the adopted child and the birth family desire and may benefit from.

On another day, on the @NerdMomMusings Twitter feed, another adoptive mom tweeted, "She is now 10, and we have always planned on telling her, but now I am not so sure."[14] She originally decided to tell her child that her father was not her biological father but goes on to explain why she's now second-guessing telling her child after a few adoptees discussed some of the struggles they faced as adoptees. I really wish comments like these were few and far between. However, in the adoption community, adoptive parents struggling with open adoptions or simply telling their children that they are adopted is still prevalent.

Is social media even the right place for these discussions? Or are adoptive parents shouting into echo chambers and only elevating the voices of other white adoptive parents?

In my experience, in some adoption groups for adoptees and adoptive parents or other social media, sometimes adoptive parents can get defensive or angry at adoptees. One parent said, "I joined the page to learn from other parents who are also involved in transracial adoption," in response to a heated discussion about politics and supporting a president who did not denounce white supremacy.[15]

Suppose you are considering joining a Facebook group or even following adoption influencers. If you do, it is vital that you curate your feeds to varied resources so that they don't just involve following more white adoptive parents who share the same viewpoint. If you are considering adoption or have adopted, you need to be willing to listen to the voices of adoptees, birth parents, and even adoptive parents of color. To do this, make sure to follow, like, and subscribe to content creators from these other parts of the adoption community. However, it is also essential that you recognize your place in that community and the impact your comments and reactions can have.

## Proper Social Media Etiquette for Adoptive Parents

Social media can either be a quick gateway to all-out arguments in comment sections or a valuable tool to foster community, discussion, and education. It can be easy to get overwhelmed in certain Facebook groups and end up replying to someone's post out of anger or defensiveness. Still, in order to remain respectful and conscientious of the power adoptive parents wield in the adoption community, it is essential to remember a few key points: 1) listen and learn from adoptee voices; 2) pause before responding and research concepts that you aren't familiar with; 3) don't respond if you cannot be respectful; and 4) be open to different perspectives.

Remember that adoptees and birth parents who are educators and content creators typically do a lot of the work that they publish on social media, blogs, and podcasts for free. The work involves a lot of emotional labor by the marginalized person, and when our time is not valued or respected by adoptive parents, it is exhausting. It can be extremely difficult for adoptees to deal with requests from adoptive parents who want answers to difficult questions that bring up personal adoption trauma and who even ask for consults about complex problems within adoptive families without offering the adoptee financial compensation for their labor and time. If you find it necessary to consult with an adoptee, or even a birth parent, with specific adoption questions, be polite, inquire about their consulting fees, and compensate them for their time.

Remember that it is important for adoptive parents to be willing to put as much time and as many resources into educating themselves as they put into paying the fees in the adoption process. Many adoptive parents spend a lot of hours doing fundraisers, working multiple jobs, and so on to afford adoption, and then after they adopt, some of them go on to complain about the expenses of therapy, mentoring, and anti-racism work that could really benefit the adopted child of color and their family.

Being willing to put in the effort to afford the post-adoption care and education that is often necessary sets a good example and shows your future adopted children that you are willing to do the work. Adhering to the four key points mentioned previously can also help you utilize social media to enhance your knowledge of cultural identity, adoptee advocacy, search and reunion, and the nuances of open and closed adoptions. If you are willing to take these steps, you can help the adoption community work together to improve some of the systemic issues and open up to discussing more nuanced issues.

## Adoption Fundraising

For birth families, who often cannot afford to raise the child they are placing for adoption, and for adoptees who know that they were placed for adoption due to financial reasons, adoption fundraising can be a sensitive subject. They can find it extremely frustrating and painful to see a prospective adoptive parent receive such support from their church, friends, family, and communities who are willing to donate money for often costly adoption fees. Fundraisers in which prospective parents are selling shirts, receiving donated gifts, and establishing GoFundMes plague the online world of adoption. Prospective adoptive parents often receive thousands of dollars of support to adopt whereas the birth mother in need receives nothing. As mentioned earlier, adoption costs typically range from $20,000 to$50,000.[16] Yet endless expectant parents face judgment, skepticism, and accusations of being drug users if they ask for help. If an expectant mother received a similar amount to what adoptive parents pay, it would be enough to hold her over until she is able to get on her feet and keep her baby if she desires to.

When I interviewed Aliyah Santos on the *Adoptee Thoughts* podcast, she shared that she experienced pressure from an agency to give her child up for adoption when she went there to see about getting help as a pregnant seventeen-year-old. She shared the following with me.

> I went to one of these houses, one of these maternity homes for help. Just to see what my options were because if she (my adoptive mother) kicked me out, I needed someplace to go. And that was one of the first things they said to me . . . If you give your child up for adoption, you won't have to worry about it anymore.[17]

*Maternity homes* are generally group homes created for pregnant women or parenting youth between the ages of sixteen and twenty-two. Depending on the home, they typically offer educational programs to teach parenting skills, child development, family budgeting, and health and nutrition.[18] In the United States, the Runaway and Homeless Youth Act was passed in 1974; it authorized the Transitional Living Program (TLP) that helped create short-term care for youth not already receiving services from child welfare or the juvenile justice system. The Maternity Group Home Program for Pregnant and Parenting Youth (MGH) was funded under the TLP via the Reconnecting Homeless Youth Act of 2008 in the hopes of promoting long-term economic independence for parenting youth.[19]

On paper, maternity homes look like a great option for mothers in need of a little help, but unfortunately, it is not uncommon for women to feel pressured to place their child for adoption in return for these services. My birth mother was admitted with her eldest son to a maternity home in Colombia when she was six months pregnant and received help for about three months. Adoption paperwork states that she received training in arts and crafts, knitting and cooking, and was set up with a job when she was dismissed from the home fifteen days postpartum. But after I talked with my birth mother this past March, I found that her story was not one full of support. She was not allowed to hold or name any of her children at birth and was repeatedly told that adoption would be the better option. Nearly thirty years after placing three of her children for adoption, she is still swamped with grief and regret.

Adoption can be beautiful if a mother chooses that option without pressure from society and if it is truly the right choice for her. On a website called Unplanned Pregnancy dedicated to providing resources for persons with unplanned pregnancies, they make it very clear that pregnant individuals should take some precautions before going to maternity homes. Some things pregnant women should consider before contacting such facilities are as follows: 1) some homes have deep religious values; others require the pregnant woman to sign a contract saying that she will carry her pregnancy to term before the facility is willing to providing housing; 2) many homes have curfews and supervision requirements; 3) some homes do put pressure on what choice the women can make during the course of the pregnancy—this is because some adoption agencies work very closely with maternity homes.[20]

This is why Aliyah's story about being pressured at a maternity home is not very surprising. Many programs tend to push the pro-adoption narrative because they see it as the best option for the child and adoptive couple, but it is often not supportive of the expectant mother. When we fail to support women in need, women who don't really *want* to choose adoption, we are just helping a crooked system that supports the privileged. I know that fifteen days after having my children I was not ready to go back to work, and because I know the struggles I faced as a married, educated woman in the United States, I cannot imagine what those of birth mothers without the support of family and friends must go through.

If you are a prospective adoptive parent looking to adopt but need the support of fundraisers, it is important to consider the painful impact they can have. Consider why churches, friends, and family are so willing to support prospective adoptive families and the impact the same amount of funds could have on family preservation. Put yourself in the shoes of the birth family or an adoptee and consider how it would make you feel if your roles were reversed. I urge prospective adoptive parents to consider alternative methods for raising funds, like taking a second job delivering food, waitressing, or even dog walking. At the very least, if you still plan to go through with raising money via fundraising, put a part of the money you raised toward family preservation.

## THE CHRISTIAN CHURCH AND ITS CONNECTION WITH ADOPTION

I have always known that the church has played a big role in the adoption industry despite it not being the primary motivator for my parents to adopt me and my brother. It's hard to miss the weight of it in prospective adoptive parents' references to adoption and in current adoptive parents' language as well. After all, the "call to adopt" is a reason many adoptive parents have decided to do so. And after discussing the role the church plays in adoption with other adoptees, I was inspired to do more research about its impact.

A premise of the Christian adoption movement is that the Bible teaches Christians to treat orphans and adoption as one connected unit. Lifeway Research conducted a survey in 2017 on churchgoers' views of adoption and foster care. The survey found that about four in ten Protestant churchgoers have been involved in adoption or foster care in the past year. Executive director of Lifeway Research, Scott McConnell, stated that it might be because "the Bible commands them to care for widows and orphans."[21]

God views orphans as a group with special concern and compassion because they are the most vulnerable and in need of assistance. This need to help children is moved by the need to provide a "father for the fatherless." Adoption is the ideal solution because it is an effective, permanent, and compassionate way to provide a family for children in need. In addition, if you look further into it, many Christians believe that every Christian is "adopted" by God. Therefore, by adopting a child into a Christian home, they are actually welcoming that child into the family of God. Emulating God's work on a microlevel within their family helps them promote adoption and encourage more families to adopt.[22]

James 1:27 states, "Religion that God our Father accepts as pure and faultless is this: to look after orphans and widows in their distress and keep oneself from being polluted by the world." In blogs by adoptive parents, many of them use this Bible verse to explain why they chose adoption. In one particular post, an adoptive mother said that she "had the capacity, through Christ, to love any child with an unconditional love."[23] Influencer Myka Stauffer, the prominent family YouTuber, said that "God softened" her and her husband's hearts and convinced her to adopt a child with special needs.[24] Arguably, their belief that faith was guiding them left them unprepared for Huxley's needs and led to rehoming him.

This prominent evangelical belief started to really take off in the 2000s when pastors encouraged pro-life families to adopt children they wanted to be born. In response, many new adoption agencies were created by churches who praised and encouraged more families to adopt. In 2009, the Southern Baptist Convention, which was the second-largest denomination at the time, directed all members to consider if God was calling on them to adopt. In 2010, Bethany Christian Services, one of the largest adoption agencies, had a 26 percent spike in the number of adoptions.[25]

When the adoption industry is heavily influenced by churches and their programs, it can be a strong driving factor for prospective adoptive parents. Commercials that call for mission trips in third-world countries emphasize the orphan crisis, which can make churchgoers feel pressured to help by adopting children in need. Just because many adoption agencies have some ties to religious organizations does not mean that those agencies are ethical; it is important to do your own research to find out if the adoption practices are ethical and actually needed.

# 5

## PARENTING YOUR ADOPTED CHILD

As a parent to two (biological) children, I have found that it can seem like parenting is, in part, a constant battle to make sure that my children are loved, educated, and protected to the best of my ability. And when I look at the world the way it is, I find it disheartening to realize that my multiracial Latino boys will have to face racism and other battles as they grow up. When we look at our children's adoring and beautiful faces, it can be a hard reality to accept that they will need to face some things on their own without our protection. But while there may not be a perfect solution to these issues, we can prepare and educate our children to become their own advocates and to become independent. I strongly believe that adoptive parents who are educated and ready to do the work can help set their children up for success.

### WHAT CAN ADOPTIVE PARENTS DO?

When considering adoption, many adoptive parents often have numerous questions; they want to know the answers to involved questions like how to nurture a strong ethnic identity in their child as a person of color, or even just the answers to basic questions that revolve around hair care or other hygiene routines. From my experience, many of these nuanced questions seem to focus on how to make the experience easier and better for the adopted child and don't take into account the complex work adoptive parents need to address within themselves. Or, at the very least, this type of question does not come up until *after* an adoption has been finalized. This is why I hope to encourage more prospective adoptive parents and current adoptive parents to take a front seat in their education before their children are old enough to advocate for themselves.

These are some questions I wish my adoptive parents had considered before they adopted. I'm not saying this to trying to stir the pot or make my parents feel guilty, but asking such questions and listening to the answers would have widened their thinking and allowed them to see how these different aspects could really affect my life as a transracial adoptee. For example, lack of racial mirrors negatively affected my self-esteem, but my parents didn't understand why or how that was a problem for me as one of the few Latinx in our community. Did they notice that most people of color in our close circles were employees? Or that practically none of their peers or close friends were people of color?

By asking more questions, you can gain a new perspective on a life that was the norm for you as a white individual—and the privilege that you may have overlooked. I have had the unique experience of being raised as if I was white. To be completely honest, I seldom thought about these questions until my adoption came to light. Then I had to reconcile with my new identity and the experiences of growing up in a white family. It allowed me to see how easy it was for me to not think about the importance of some of these issues when, at the time, they were not affecting me personally. After all, I loved and treated everyone the same despite their race/gender/sexuality. I was a *good* person. But the thing is, I may have been a good person, but I was also naïve. I didn't really see how being a lone person of color in a sea of white friends, relatives, and teachers could be so isolating. I didn't realize how being quiet when other people in my life were openly racist made me complacent in racism.

*Would they have been happy with just any child? Would they have chosen me if given a choice? Would their family have had problems with a child of a different race? How would they deal with racism? Why did they feel color didn't matter?*

Their answers to these questions became very important to me as I processed being adopted and they affected how I viewed myself. Knowing that my parents chose to adopt me from Colombia because it was the first type of adoption they heard about that would not require contact with my birth mother left a bad taste in my mouth. If they had been prepared and had taken the time to think through some of the answers to these questions before talking to me, they might have realized how hurtful some of their answers would be. They could have saved us both a lot of pain and frustration. This is why I encourage all prospective adoptive parents to ask themselves the following questions:

### Questions Adoptive Parents Need to Ask Themselves Before Adopting

- What kind of anti-racist work am I involved in?
- Are my interactions with people of color sincere?
- How many people of color are in my inner circles?
  - ▸ Friends
  - ▸ Family

- ▶ Schools

- ▶ Mom group

- ▶ Book groups

- ▶ Gym

- Do I have any family members who hold racist beliefs?

- Do I have family members with biased beliefs?

- Do I have racist or prejudiced beliefs?

- Name an example of current and past biases.

- Am I willing to speak up against prejudiced family members and friends?

- Do I live in a diverse area?

- Am I willing to move to a diverse area so my child can have racial mirrors?

- Why am I choosing to adopt a child of a different race/ethnicity than mine?

- Does part of the reason have to do with the extra time I'd have to wait if I only wanted to adopt a white child?

- Why do I think there are more children of color up for adoption?

- What words would I use to describe a birth mother? What do I think they look like?

- Am I comfortable with an open adoption? Why or why not?

- Will I be comfortable explaining my choices to my child one day?

Although you will need to do a lot of work internally or with your spouse/partner, you can also use the resources in Chapter 9 to help guide you with the next steps after you answer these questions for yourself. I also highly recommend that adoptive parents start going to therapy before they adopt and after. As humans, our life experiences and how we were raised definitely impact how we parent. Working with a therapist is a great first step to making sure you do not bring your own intergenerational trauma into future parenting decisions and methods.

As I mention throughout the book, to grow as an adoptive parent, you must be willing to *do the work* and spend some time doing further research. Simply reading one book or having a few conversations with other adoptees or adoptive parents is not enough. The work of being a parent, and especially an adoptive parent, is ongoing.

You *will* make mistakes.

I know that is hard to hear. But as a mother, I've learned that it is okay to make mistakes as long as you are willing to learn from them. Don't be afraid to be humble, to apologize to your children, or even to admit that you don't know all the answers. Showing your children, biological or adopted, that you are willing to go the extra mile to learn and help them to the best of your ability will make all the difference in the world.

I come from an adoptive family that has had its fair share of ups and downs, and I can honestly tell you that my relationship with my mother has never been better—all because we both took the time to work together to listen and to learn from our experiences. If you want to learn more about our relationship, check out our interview on the podcast, *Do the Work* (a Three Uncanny Four production), called "Family Secrets: Melissa & Paula," by searching the name on any podcast platform.

## GOOD INTENTION, BAD OUTCOMES

From my experience with adoptive parents, many times, they have the best intentions—to help protect their kids from being

teased or feeling different. But unfortunately, you can do everything right, and your adopted child may *still* struggle.

Aversion to discomfort is normal; it is natural for humans to
avoid topics that make us uncomfortable. But frankly, as adoptive parents, it is your responsibility to make yourself uncomfortable in order to learn. If we, as humans, are comfortable 100
percent of the time, we are not motivated to learn and grow.

As parents to children of color, here are some hard truths
that you will have to face:

- Your child will experience racism.

- Your child may never be 100 percent comfortable
  with their place in your family.

- They may not like the image of themselves they see in
  the mirror.

- They may hate being adopted.

- They may dislike telling others that they have white
  parents.

- There are no guarantees. You can do everything right,
  and your child may still struggle.

This list can go on and on. But once you acknowledge the
darker side of adoption, you can become more empathetic and
involved in your child's life and you can support them as much
as possible. Adoptees need unconditional love from their parents, like all children. Adoptees need to know that we can be
angry, sad, frustrated, and tell our parents how we feel in order
to process and grow as people.

Often adoptive parents seem to have an overreaching need
to fix things for their child. But the unfortunate reality is that
adopted children will, at times, feel isolated, angry, or sad. And
despite adoptive parents' desire for a quick fix, there is none.
For example, a common question I receive in my messages from

adoptive parents is how to make their adopted child feel less alone. Adoptees say that even with some racial mirrors in their community, being the only child of color in their family makes them feel lonely. Often, adoptive parents will quickly follow up this question by asking if adopting another child from the same country will "fix" the problem.

My answer to this second question is always an unequivocal no. It will not fix the problem. There are no quick fixes to the complexities and loss that is ever-present in adoption. Adopting multiple children of color may help to a small degree, but often, I wholeheartedly believe, it will not be the solution adoptive parents think it will be. I and many other transracial adoptees I know who have siblings from the same country feel similar isolation to those without siblings, and this is because no two adoptees are alike. And while adding another child of the same race will physically make your family more diverse, no two children will feel the same way about adoption. It is not uncommon for adopted siblings to have very different opinions and trauma from adoption that they may not be willing to share with each other.

## WHAT PROSPECTIVE ADOPTIVE PARENTS CAN DO

The questions many current adoptees get from hopeful adoptive parents are something like these: "I'm thinking about adopting, how can I make sure my adoptee is okay and doesn't have any issues?" or "You seemed to have turned out okay, what can I do that your parents did?"

I hate to break it to you, but there is no secret formula for raising an adopted child. Just like there is no secret formula for raising biological children. You can do everything right and your child may still develop a mental illness, act out in school, or have problems with drugs—just like biological children.

After all, part of raising humans is realizing that there is no perfect formula to prevent unsavory outcomes that you would prefer to avoid. Children grow up to become adult humans with varied life experiences and genetics that shape them into the people that they are.

Current research suggests that transracial adoptive parents are capable of fostering an adoptee's healthy ethnic identity development. However, studies still suggest that adoptive parents may not always recognize the prevalence of racism in their children's lives and may make fewer attempts to address racial bias. Parents who have experienced higher levels of adoption stigma are more likely to have less of a colorblind mentality, which may put them in a better position to recognize and validate their adoptee's experiences as a person of color.[1]

I recently interviewed a transracial adoptee, Louise, who had a wonderful experience with her adoptive parents. After she was born, her birth mother and her adoptive mother shared almost a month of time together before she was taken to Australia with her adoptive family, and afterward, she had a very open adoption. She had a wonderful relationship with her adoptive mother and even felt comfortable inviting her on a trip to Indonesia during her second visit with her birth mother.

I feel that Louise's experience is important to talk about because her (adoptive) mother did all the "right" things. She integrated her child's birth culture, she talked about racism, and she continued to have a dialogue with her child as she learned more about racism throughout the years. And yet, in our interview, Louise divulged that she still struggles with her identity as an adult, and even now, as a mother, she has a difficult time figuring out where she fits between her birth culture and her adoptive culture.

*I feel like I should be loyal to my birth country and birth mother, but I'm very loving and grateful for my adoptive family. I spent*

*so many years thinking am I brown? Am I white? Am I Indo-*
*nesian? Am I Australian? I had assimilated and camouflaged*
*myself so much that it definitely flavored how I am as a person.*
*I felt shame that I was abandoning my roots.*[2]

Louise had a happy childhood as an adoptee and had a good
relationship with her adoptive parents. Yet, even so, she still
struggles when trying to reconnect to her birth culture and
when talking about race with other relatives; often, she still feels
whitewashed.

Quotes from interviews on my podcast stand out to me:

*The way adoption is marketed was part of the reason I felt so*
*isolated. Because whenever I tried to research anything about*
*adoption, it was always White parents with smiling, Asian chil-*
*dren. And I thought . . . That's not how I feel. Is there some-*
*thing wrong with me? Why doesn't anyone look like they feel*
*like I do?*[3]

*I should not hold in my own feelings about what I'm thinking*
*and how I'm feeling, especially when it is tied to my culture,*
*tied to my community, because they (my parents) are not going*
*to experience that. And that's the thing, and for all adoptees*
*listening . . . your parents will not experience your race through*
*you. They won't. There's no connection; there's no possible way*
*to feel all of what you're feeling because they're not your race.*[4]

It is important to remember that adoption stories are never
black and white. There are no definitive answers to a perfect
childhood and perfect development. Adoptees' lives are unique,
complicated, beautiful, and sometimes tragic.

As parents, we often have a desire to protect our children
from all pain, but we know it is impossible to prevent all the
struggles they may face as they grow up. What we can do instead
is try our best, acknowledge our mistakes, and learn from them.
That said, there are things you can do to lessen the likelihood

that your adoptive child will have issues with substance abuse or mental illness and that will allow you to just raise a well-adjusted child. Let's first talk about resiliency.

When I was taking psychology courses in my freshman year of college, one of the first things I learned was that children had very high *resiliency*. What does that mean? Well, it means that they are developing an ability to overcome serious hardship; the more resilient you are, the lower the risk of developing a psychiatric disorder.[5] The problem is that adopted children are intrinsically subjected to trauma the moment they are separated from their biological parents, particularly their mother, very early on. So, when something else happens later, like experiencing a bully, or having their adoptive parents divorce, it can hit them harder than expected. As adoptees, we need a safe place to process our trauma without being subjected to judgment for having feelings; we often experience many traumatic and stressful events that can inhibit our resilience.

Now, this does not mean adopted children should be able to run free, break all the rules and laws, and get in trouble. As I previously mentioned, adoptees have a higher likelihood of developing certain mental illnesses, like oppositional defiant disorder, ADHD, and anxiety, to name a few, and this should be taken into consideration when parenting.[6] For instance, typical punishments for children, like being sent to their room, can be counterproductive and even harmful for adopted children. Many adoptees have a deep-rooted fear of abandonment; it is important to consider this when coming up with suitable and appropriate repercussions for misbehavior.[7] Try time-ins, extra chores with the family, time spent volunteering, and so on.

When it comes to transracial adoption, white adoptive parents typically use four cultural socialization strategies: cultural assimilation, enculturation, racial inculturation, and child's choice. *Cultural assimilation* requires the minimum effort from the adoptive parents because the children are already exposed to the majority culture. A different variant of this strategy emphasizes colorblindness and deemphasizes the child's birth culture. *Enculturation* is when adoptive parents provide their children with social, educational, and cultural opportunities to instill ethnic awareness and to promote a positive ethnic identity. *Racial inculturation* is when adoptive parents teach their children to deal with discrimination and racism effectively. And *child's choice* is a recent strategy in which adoptive parents initially provide cultural opportunities, but then adjust their efforts based on the child's wishes.[8]

Adoptive parents and prospective adoptive parents can take many concrete actions to make positive changes in the adoption community that help all parts of the triad. For instance, a consistent, supportive, primary caregiver is often the most valuable tool in strengthening a child's resiliency. One of the most important characteristics of such caregivers is that they have open minds and hearts and are willing to truly listen to adoptees' lived experiences.

## Active Listening

When you are an *active listener*, you sit back and show that you believe the voices of adoptees and birth parents that hold different views on adoption and that these voices have value to you. This means you hold back on responding to posts on social media, commenting on podcasts or YouTube videos, or responding in person in any way that invalidates those adoptees' or birth parents' lived experiences. When you become an adoptive parent, you have to recognize your privilege in the triad and realize that in adoption, your experience is and will continue to be very different from those of adoptees and birth parents. That doesn't mean you have to change every thought you have and agree with everything others say about adoption. It means that you should value the emotional labor that those people are putting in by publicly discussing their experiences and views on adoption . . . especially if you were the one who asked them questions or if they were spurred on to react by a comment that you made.

Instead of responding right away when something intrigues you, frustrates you, or makes you sad, step away from everything and take a breath, go on a walk, read a book—anything to separate yourself from the heated emotions that you are feeling. If you are in a heated discussion with someone, stepping back gives both you and the other person the respect you need to learn from what the other is saying. Take some time to conduct some research if you are unsure or disagree with them. Then, if you are still frustrated and confused, ask questions in an appropriate setting or with a counselor or an adoptee advocate. Remember that if you are asking an adoptee for guidance, ask them their rates, and pay them for their time. You can also look up podcasts/videos online to learn about topics like white fragility and toxic positivity in adoption and be willing to sit in your new knowledge until your fight-or-flight instinct calms down enough for you to actually grow from the experience.

If you want to raise transracial adoptees or are already parents of transracial adoptees, you need to be as prepared as possible to answer their hard questions. To teach them about racism, to integrate their culture, to not judge their birth families, and most importantly . . . to listen to them and validate their feelings when the world would silence them as being ungrateful.

## Embrace Your Own Racial Identity

Acknowledging your race is not inherently bad, although our society has made it seem almost taboo to bring it up. If you, as an adoptive parent, find it difficult to embrace your own racial identity as a white person, how are you going to show your children that it is important for them to embrace their own as people of color? It can be more difficult to see white privilege and how problematic it can be if you often assume that white people are the default race that should be present in movies, books, and media.

Children often learn by modeling, so it is essential that you model the conversations you want your children to have in order for them to explore their identities.

Embrace what being a white person means in our society and engage in conversations about your culture and the privileges it may grant you. You can start by sharing family recipes that you cherish during holiday meals, music you listen to, or even your favorite sports. These are all typical ways families share traditions or important aspects of their lives, and by discussing your own, you may help your child become interested in both their adoptive and biological family's traditions.

When you have conversations about privilege or systemic racism, please remember to be aware of your tone and word choice, because kids pick up on everything. If you aren't ready to give it your all, practice these conversations with a partner before engaging in them with your kids. It is important to refrain from blaming or guilting one another, to use these discussions to explore and validate everyone's experiences.

Here is a list of questions you can use to start up conversations with your spouse and other family or friends.

### Conversation Starters:

- How often do you think of your race or ethnicity?
- What part of your racial or ethnic identity makes you proud?
- Have you ever experienced being treated differently because of your race/ethnicity?

- Have you ever witnessed someone else being treated differently due to their race/ethnicity? How did it make you feel?

- Do you ever have to think about your race/ethnicity before you make any daily decisions?

- Have you ever been the only one of your race/ethnicity in school, at work, or at a large gathering? How did it make you feel?

- How frequently do you engage with people of a different race or ethnic background?

## Be Willing to Promote Opposite Views

For every positive story of an "abandoned baby" meeting their adoptive parents that you share on social media or talk about with your family/friends, be willing to do the same with less-positive experiences of adoption. This involves work. If you are unwilling to put in the time and effort to educate your family and friends on how multidimensional adoption is, then you still have work to do as an adoptive parent. Because, as a transracial adoptee, I can tell you that from research and from my own personal experience, your adopted child will have some negative feelings toward adoption at some point in their life. And if you are unwilling to discuss this other reality of adoption or simply read or watch a video about another way of looking at things posted by a stranger, you will be unprepared to accept and validate your own child's feelings when/if they arise.

If, the majority of the time, you refuse to consume media that depicts the nuances of adoption and simply absorb positive stories, you are not ready to adopt transracially. You are not ready to face the challenges that will arise. You are not ready to give a transracial adoptee all that they need.

So, how can you prepare so that you are ready?

Start by looking for essays, books, and podcasts by transracial adoptees. Take in and really listen to what they have to say. Bookmark topics that you don't understand or that you disagree with and dig into why you think the way you do. This is a great way to learn how to respect your child's views on adoption as they grow up and mature, and it is also a wonderful introduction to cultural immersion.

## Cultural Immersion: Developing and Maintaining Cultural Competency

When adoptees advocate for adoptive families to promote cultural immersion within our families, we mean that we want adoptive parents heavily involved in the process of immersion as well. Sending your children to cultural camps, foreign language classes, diverse schools, and so on, are all good first steps. But they aren't enough. If you're an adoptive parent and you aren't involved in learning about your child's culture, participating in hands-on ways, learning the language, using it at home, going and volunteering at culture camps, cooking traditional recipes at home, listening to the music—can you truly say that you have prioritized cultural competency in your household?

One of the first things I learned in my undergraduate psychology program was that children easily learn from parents modeling behavior. The saying, "monkey see, monkey do," is a common phrase in parents' vocabulary for a reason. To make this work for yourself and your family, start by volunteering with the cultural camps, by taking language classes by yourself, by making recipes for the entire family to enjoy, and by listening to the music that is prominent in your child's birth culture.

It is beyond frustrating for adoptees to hear things like adoptive parents saying that they do not have enough money to travel back to their child's birth country. Think about it: adoptive parents will move heaven and earth to get through the adoption process as efficiently as possible. In order to be able to afford to adopt, they'll create GoFundMes, sell T-shirts, get their community and church involved, and so on, but when it is suggested that they incorporate trips to birth countries, move to a more diverse area, hire language tutors, or take advantage of other important tools for cultural immersion, it seems as if many adoptive parents are unable to devote just as much passion and effort to providing these important experiences and avenues to their children.

As parents, it is easy to become overwhelmed with the many tasks we need to do. But as adoptive parents, teaching cultural competency to your children of color is just as vital as teaching them basic hygiene. Developing cultural competency is essential to the prosperous development that transracial adoptees need to help us understand our identity, and one of the best ways to start developing this is for adoptive parents to expand their circle of racial mirrors.

Another way to expand on this learned cultural competency is to find groups of international and transracial adoptees to expose your child to. The impact of being in a roomful of adoptees who understand the struggles and even the joys of being adopted is unparalleled. When I interviewed Jessica Luciere for episode 5 of my podcast, *Adoptee Thoughts*, she said that "When you walk into a room [full of adoptees], no one is wondering. . . everyone has a similar narrative, more or less. Nobody essentially looks like their parents. I mean, we have some people who do, just by happenstance, but that in itself sets the tone. There's an instant acceptance."[9]

## Expanding Your Circle of Racial Mirrors

You've probably heard the term *racial mirror* referred to in the adoption community. A racial mirror refers to people who share the same race and ethnicity as you.

What you may not know is that the type of racial mirrors that you expose your children of color to is important. If done properly, you are helping them explore and form a strong identity as a person of color. If the racial mirrors they have are not diverse, however, exposure can actually be detrimental.

Let me give you an example. Say you are well-off and employ a maid, driver, and lawn staff, all of whom are your child's racial mirrors. If the only racial mirrors your child sees are "the help," this can reinforce some prevalent and negative stereotypes that your child is already exposed to in the media. It is essential to expand the mirrors around your child to include people from all walks of life. Seek mentors who are doctors, entrepreneurs, and librarians, in addition to those who may work manual labor jobs, so that your child can broaden their circle and see that BIPOC can work at various professions, and be in different economic situations and lifestyles.

# 6

# SEARCH AND REUNION

et's talk about an adoptee's right to have access to their
original birth certificates and to establish a connection
to their birth family. In the United States and many
other countries, in the first half of the twentieth century it
became standard for such records to be sealed because of the
stigma that was commonly attached to being an adoptee and
the worry that children would be considered illegitimate. In
Western Australia, laws were tightened to restrict access to
such records in 1921, and in the Soviet Union, adoption laws
were tightened in the 1960s. It wasn't until 1975 in Wales
and England that children over eighteen were allowed to
access their original birth certificates. In the United States,
many states still require a court order to gain access to these
documents.[1]

Despite this difficulty, you may find that in closed adoptions,
your child may still decide that they need to search. And when
they decide to find their birth family, it is natural for it to bring

up feelings of insecurity, jealousy, and even anger in the adoptive parent and adopted child. This time in our lives is special
and terrifying, but it is hard enough on adoptees without the
added pressure of keeping our adoptive parents happy. Some
adoptees, like me, may even feel that thinking about their birth
or birth mother makes them feel ungrateful to our adoptive parents. I believe that it is the adoptive parent's responsibility to
support their child with the decision to search as long as no
present threat of danger will result from reconnecting with the
birth family.

To make this process easier on your adoptee, try to refrain
from making negative comments about your child's birth family
in front of them. Similarly, try not to express jealousy or anger
toward their birth parents. And whatever you do, do not make
it about you. From my personal experience beginning such a
search, I can tell you that I was conflicted almost every step of
the way. I felt like I had to downplay my excitement and desire
to find my birth family and instead emphasize my need for medical information. This weighed heavily on my heart during every
step of the process, and I often felt guilt for even wanting to
search in the first place.

To help adoptive parents remember what behaviors are
helpful versus what behaviors can be detrimental when their
child searches, I have created lists of what to do and what not
to do. These lists are based on my personal experience as an
adult adoptee, so although they can serve as a guide for adoptive
parents, be sure to edit them to suit your family's needs. For
example, if your child is underage when they begin a search for
biological relatives, you may need to make some changes to how
they communicate and how to handle in-person meetings for
safety reasons.

| WHAT NOT TO DO | WHAT TO DO |
|---|---|
| • Do not make their search about yourself. | • Love your child unconditionally and support them with their decision to search unless they are in danger. |
| • Do not make your child feel guilty. | • Tell them you love them. |
| • Do not insult your child's birth family. | • Ask them questions if they seem open to sharing. |
| • Do not bring up the adoptive parent's personal history with law/drugs/homelessness. | • Encourage an emotional outlet (i.e., journaling, music, painting). |
| • Do not pressure your child to share every detail. | • Help them find an adoption-competent therapist if they are interested. |
| • Do not pressure your child to include you on calls or visits. | • Ask them if they would like your input or assistance. |

Adoptees often feel the need to connect with our roots as a part of our journey of self-discovery and as a process of understanding our identity, and it can be heartbreaking to have our (adoptive) parents seem to be against that. We often just want our parents' unconditional love and support to explore our birth families, which is why it's important for adoptive parents to realize that our need to search does not set up a competition between adoptive and birth parents. Children, even adult children, can love many parents at the same time. Our need to search does not mean we are trying to replace anyone; we're just trying to add more pieces to the puzzle that is our family.

Additionally, if you feel the need to begin your own search for your child's birth family before they are old enough to share their thoughts and preferences, I suggest that you consider what you know about the health of the birth family. If there are no known medical issues, is there any reason you cannot wait for your child's input on such a search? If you do need to search for the medical history of your adopted child's family, do your best to limit your search to just medical parameters. If you have no other pressing reason, wait another year or two, and then ask your child if they want to search. Additionally, are you respecting the birth family's wishes by searching and trying to maintain contact? Keep in mind what you agreed to when your adoption contract was drawn up. Search and reunion are complicated enough when the adoptee decides to do the search on their own, but for an adoptive parent to search without their child's input is something that can easily go from well intentioned to crossing boundaries.

Lastly, if you have decided to search against your child's wishes because you believe they are too young to make such a decision, I urge you to put yourself in their shoes. Adoptees have so many decisions made for them by others, they deserve to have some authority over this part of their lives. If you still decide to move forward, consider keeping records, photos, letters, and information related to your child's adoption in a box where they can access age-appropriate information when they are ready. Do not push an adoptee to make contact if they are against it; be patient, and consider working closely with a counselor specializing in adoption, child development, and/or trauma.

## MY REUNION STORY

When reunions with birth families are displayed in the media, they often include lots of tears and a happily-ever-after fadeout that leaves the rest of the experience to the viewer's imagination. It is important to note that reunions can be as complex as they are wonderful, and some even end in heartbreak.

When I began searching for my birth mom for the first time, I had no idea what I was doing. I looked up my birth mother's name on Facebook and tried to Google her. I was in the beginning stages of grief after finding out I was adopted and felt that I *needed* to know who my birth parents were to figure out who I was. Looking back at those first attempts, I know that I wasn't ready. When I found her, years later, I was in a much better place to digest the relationship and set up boundaries. At that point, I had been in therapy for years, had read about other adoptees' experiences with reunion, and had even reconnected with two half-siblings before I really tried to find my mom.

I initially dove headfirst into the idea of a reunion because I was desperate for a connection with my birth family. When I found my siblings, the fact that I never considered how our different upbringings and baggage would affect our reunion never crossed my mind until things quickly didn't work out the way I imagined they would. There was no fairytale ending. If anything, our relationship took more work than the others in my life because of so many lost years. My hopes and expectations were too high, and both sides had not prepared enough for what an emotionally charged situation reunions can be.

Emailing back and forth with a sister for the first time was something news broadcasts and movies hadn't prepared either of us for. After a difficult beginning, my sisters and I agreed to take some time to work on ourselves before slowly getting to know each other a year later. Taking that time and space allowed us to work on our own trauma due to adoption, and we now have a much stronger and happier relationship.

After learning from that experience, I knew to set certain expectations and boundaries when I reconnected with my birth mom. By giving myself the time to reflect on what I wanted from the relationship and what I was comfortable with, I was better prepared. This is why I encourage adoptive parents to have open conversations with their children where they can encourage them to think about some of the following questions, before jumping headfirst into a reunion with certain expectations.

### Questions Adoptees Should Ask Themselves Before Reconnecting with a Birth Relative:

- What do I want from this relationship?
- Do I want to meet in person?
- How often do I want to communicate? What type of communication do I want to use?
- Am I willing to send money home?
- Will I be heartbroken if my relative doesn't want a relationship? Have I prepared myself enough to handle that?
- Am I able to set boundaries if my relative wants more than I'm prepared to give?
- Do I have a support system?
- What do I *need* to know, versus what do I just *want* to know?
- Can I afford a translator?

I made the preceding list of questions and considerations in my journal before I even considered moving forward with my search for my birth mother. After a few days of really considering the possible negative outcomes of a reunion, I felt that I was ready for anything. I had thought about what I'd do and how I'd react if I found out that my mom had passed away, or that she wouldn't want or couldn't have a relationship with me for whatever reason. I had even decided that I wasn't ready for an open relationship. My focus this time was mostly on health issues due to some pressing health concerns I had for myself and my child. Had this reunion been my first connection with biological relatives, I don't think I would have been ready for the rollercoaster of emotions that it caused.

Having concrete answers to these questions I had written down allowed me to figure out my priorities and how I would handle different situations. They even pushed me to really consider if I was ready to search. Each journey with search and reunion is deeply personal, and often, there are no right and wrong answers. You and your child need to figure out what is healthiest for you while trying to be respectful to the other people involved.

Curiosity about our family is natural, but adoptees may not have access to a way to establish communication with our birth families. We may find it useful to write down a list of important questions that we want or need to address first. This is especially important if the adoptee doesn't think their birth mother can or will be able to talk to them. For instance, when I reconnected with my birth mother, we could only talk through a third party since I didn't speak Spanish well enough, and she hadn't told her husband and other children about my sisters and me. Many women who have placed children can be in tricky situations and may not be able to be as open as they would like with their child who found them; it can require some serious understanding and sympathy from all parties to work through this challenge.

In order to make this transition easier, it can be great to encourage your child to create a list of questions that they can ask their birth parent quickly so they don't forget something important that they wanted to know. You can also share the following list with the investigator or other third party that may be helping with the search so they can ask on your behalf.

**Questions Adoptees May Have for a Birth Parent:**

- Who is my birth father?
- Did you hold me?
- Was I breastfed?
- How could you leave me?
- Why did you choose adoption?
- What do you look like?
- Is there any medical history that I need to be aware of?
- Are you okay?
- Do you think about me?
- Will you take a DNA test?

Birth parents are people. They go on to have lives that include new jobs, marriage, and even other children. As adoptees, it can be hard to imagine our birth parents moving on after placing us for adoption, but I found it helpful to remember that moving on does not mean forgetting, and my birth mother's journey is not a reflection on my worth as a person. Birth parents are allowed to have families and experiences, and I would never want my birth mother or father to simply live the rest of their lives in pain because they chose adoption. But knowing this does not erase the pain that an adoptee may feel when they hear about the family their birth parent kept.

It's important to let your adopted child know that it is okay to be angry and even jealous. But in order to heal, it is important to work through those emotions; otherwise, they cannot have a healthy relationship. And if you are an adoptee reading this, I urge you to consider how you might react if you find out that your birth mother has more children before you move forward in a search. And if, at any point, you (the adoptee) feel overwhelmed, know that is okay to step back and reevaluate before moving on. Here is a quick list of reminders that adoptive parents can share with their child to show support.

### Some Ways Adoptive Parents Can Support Their Adopted Child

- Let them know that it's okay for them to decide how much communication they are comfortable with.

- Remind them that it is okay to feel numb, sad, and angry.

- Remind them that it is normal to feel jealous of siblings their birth mother raised.

- Remind them that it's okay to be cautious and not to trust the relationship right away, or ever.

- Remind them that it is normal to be nervous about talking to you (their adoptive parents) about their birth family.

Even though I was more prepared to find my birth family this time around, I dreaded the moment when I had to tell my (adoptive) parents about my search. I was afraid we'd argue and we'd all end up angry and resentful. So, when I began the final search for my birth mother, I decided not to tell my adoptive family about it until I was ready to make contact.

After all, I knew the situation could go either way with my parents. They could be completely supportive, or they could be dismissive and defensive. Remember that it is the adoptee's decision whether or not to share this journey with their adoptive parents. Do not pressure your child to share every little detail unless they want to. What you can do is encourage them to build a support network and if it doesn't include you (their adoptive parents), that is okay.

I ended up waiting a few months after my reunion with my birth mother to tell my (adoptive) parents. Right when I found my birth mother, my father found out that he had cancer, and I was afraid he would feel that I was replacing him. I was also worried that the knowledge would be another element of stress in my mom's life that she didn't need. Waiting allowed me to process everything without navigating their reactions at the same time. When I eventually told them, the experience was, thankfully, for the most part, uneventful. However, even so, there were still a few things that they did that I appreciated, and some that I wish they had never said.

The best thing that my father did was to support me unconditionally. At times he seemed almost as excited as I was, and he was ready to help me book a trip to visit my family the moment I wanted to. I loved that he was interested in learning more and that he encouraged me to continue talking with my birth family; it showed me that he cared about me so much that knowing about them was also important to him. My dad's support for me in reconnecting with my birth family was one of the best things he gave me as an adoptive parent, and I will always cherish the moments when we talked about finding them and the interest he showed in seeing pictures and hearing their stories before he passed away.

Despite my dad's enthusiasm, however, my mom had some reservations. I could tell from the start that she wasn't super excited or necessarily supportive of me finding my birth family. I couldn't help but feel hurt that she was distant from this part of me that felt so important, even though I knew that it was probably because she was very protective of me as her only daughter. It made me feel like I had to tip-toe around what information I could share with her because I did not want to hurt her feelings.

Another difficulty that I didn't expect to face was the judgment of some of my adoptive family members. For example, some relatives actively judged my birth mother's decision to place two of my siblings and me for adoption. This was extremely painful to deal with as an adoptee, and I encourage all adoptive parents to abstain from judgment and keep certain thoughts to themselves. It can be extremely stressful for adoptees to toe the line between their families, to not hurt anyone's feelings, and also to prevent themselves from feeling guilty about wanting to search. The more adoptive parents do to support our decision to reconnect, the easier the experience can be.

# 7

# INTERVIEWS WITH ADULT TRANSRACIAL ADOPTEES

One day, as I was scrolling through Facebook, a post in one of my adoption groups caught my eye. A fellow adoptee was asking for advice on how to integrate their birth culture with parenting their child. Many adult adoptees were not exposed to our birth culture very much, and so when I saw this post, my mind went to the various responses that I typically share with adoptive parents—the checklist of options and moves for becoming more culturally competent, like integrating food, music, and traditions from their child's culture. But when I took a second to sit with my response, I started thinking about my family's efforts, the steps I had taken with my own children . . . and inevitably, I had to admit that I wasn't doing as much as I could.

This was not because I didn't want to, but because it was painful. Every time I tried to integrate cultural elements into my parenting, I felt a bit like a fraud. I didn't know how to cook Colombian meals. Hell, I didn't even know how to cut a plantain properly. The first few times I attempted that, I ended up cutting my fingers and was left with a fruit that was more dilapidated than the playdough my sons played with. I refused to speak Spanish at home for the most part because my pronunciation was horrible, and I felt awkward and unsure with the foreign words in my mouth . . . and all of this hurt. It hurt to fail at something that was supposed to be a part of my upbringing—that could have been if the cards had just been dealt a little differently.

My curiosity got the better of me, and I couldn't help but pose the adoptee's question on Twitter. As I faced some of these thoughts about my own parenting, I wondered whether other adoptees encountered similar parenting struggles because they were adopted.[1] Here are some of the answers I received:

*Too much to say! I've been obsessive about things (breastfeeding, attachment parenting) to the detriment of my health & relationships at times. But that said, I worked hard to let my kids fly by addressing my psych issues. They are both independent teens. But I feel like I paid a price. Actually, it wasn't quite like "I paid a price." Or it was a temporary & voluntary paid price! More that it was harder work than it needed to be because I so wanted to be closely attached & couldn't rely on it happening naturally, if that makes sense. It was my highest priority.*

—Kim P.

*This is a big one for me! You can probably guess I couldn't do controlled crying with my kids . . . I'm also pretty crappy with boundaries, which causes challenges. Love my babies so much though.*

—Daisy W.

*These questions are too big to answer in a tweet! One thing that I totally did not expect was being shocked by their non-adopted privilege, the things they take for granted. (Knowing their birth story and who/where they come from, to start.)*

—Colson P.

*Not knowing our biology and what was genetic or ok—over-compensating to make everything alright for them—not having a parent to tell me what to expect, to reassure, or encourage, however, determined to break cycles and accept them for them and my three girls and I are close, etc.*

—Melinda M.

*I struggle with wondering how to be an authentic parent within my personality and values, which is very distinct from my Adoptive mom's personality and values. I don't/can't parent like her . . . but her example is still my default.*

—Gemma S.

As you can tell, the answers to this question were complex; it was eye-opening to see just how much adoption affects any adoptee in any part of our lives. What I found most interesting was that many adoptees seemed to cherish the bond with their biological children almost reverently. For many of us, when our children were born was the first time we were in the same house with a biological relative and with someone who looked like us.

After reading the honest and heartfelt answers, I knew it would be essential to include an interview with other transracial adoptees in this book, not only to help support the need for more resources for transracial adoptees but to elevate the voices of adoptees of color—to show the adoption community that our voices matter and that adoptive parents can learn a lot from us.

In the following pages, I have curated a list of questions that I asked fifty transracial adoptees in an anonymous survey. I want to add that it was difficult to find adoptees who were willing to take the time to answer questions about their adoption, even though the answers were anonymous. But as an author who frequently works with other adoptees, I can understand the reluctance. Many adoptees who speak openly and honestly about their adoption can experience negative remarks from friends, family, and society.

As you go through these pages, I urge you to sit with each adoptee's answers. Then ask yourself, what are you currently doing to help your children? What can you do better? For more guidance, make sure to check out the Q&A guide at the end of this chapter.

## —— ADOPTEE SURVEY QUESTIONS AND ANONYMOUS ANSWERS ——

*All names have been changed for anonymity.*

**When did you first realize you were of a different race/ethnicity than your parents?**

*When I was 3–4 years old, my [adoptive] mom was picking me up from pre-k in Topeka, Kansas. This was in the 90s when the Phelps family was all over Topeka. They were picketing my pre-k. Fred Phelps (yes, that Phelps) called me a slur, and my mom a slur-lover. This was one of my earliest and most formative memories surrounding my race and otherness.*

—ANDREW H.

*As young as I can remember, my parents made sure I knew as early as possible.*

—TINA K.

**Did being a transracial adoptee affect your childhood in any significant way? Please explain.**

*Yes . . . because in the late 60s–early 70s . . .Belgians didn't see many Asian in [sic] "real" and we used to be seen as chink, monkey.*

—ANDREW H.

*Yes, I was whitewashed.*

—BEN C.

*Yes, I grew up in Kansas. I was one of the only people of color in my school for just about the entirety of my k–12 experience. I was also likely [one of] the only transracial adoptees, if not the only, in my school. I felt isolated and alone. When teachers were racist to me, nobody believed me. I was disciplined more often and in more extreme ways than my white peers. I also had few friends of color or role models. I felt like I was the one brown person on my lonely island.*

—KIM L.

*Yes—I did not have racial mirrors and, therefore, never created a positive self-image. I was not given the opportunity to connect with my culture or learn about myself in a way that would be necessary to develop self-respect and self-love.*

—DONNA P.

*Yes, embarrassed to bring other kids home or have them meet my family in fear of being asked a million adoption questions or being made fun of for being different since I didn't know any other adoptees, so I never had a lot of play dates with friends at my house.*

—SELENA W.

*Yea. I was raised in complete whiteness; I was bullied because of my race, and I didn't understand why or even what was going on.*

—TIM M.

*I didn't have any friends who looked like me but luckily didn't face any microaggressions or racist names as a kid. I was adopted into a Jewish family, so I was raised an Asian Jew, which was rare for my community.*

—LOGAN R.

## Did your adoptive parents integrate your birth culture? If so, how?

*Not at all. My mother wanted me all to herself and couldn't care less about what "color" I was. She was very colorblind indeed.*

—BOB Y.

*Yeah. But not well. It was good when we were younger by going to Chinese cultural events etc. But as we got older, we got busier and just ate at Chinese restaurants and called it good. But us kids needed more.*

—TAMMY S.

*Never—we never ate the food, talked about the country, or addressed that I was from another country. My parents are kind, but they don't see color; therefore, didn't see my differences.*

—VINCENT A.

*My adoptive Mother's partner is Ethiopian, it is Ethiopia every day no matter where we are, we do have a vacation home in Ethiopia, everyone in the family does speak Amharic, and I had to go to all Ethiopia parties and language classes when younger. I know how to culture switch into habesha.*

—MICHELLE P.

## How do you feel about adoption fundraising? (Adoptive parents raising funds for adoption costs via GoFundMe, etc.)

*Absolutely not. It makes me feel like you are "buying" your child, and no child wants to feel like they were bought and can be returned. As the goal for the fundraiser is to buy something like team uniforms for a sports team. I think adoption funding should be a personal financial goal for the family. If one parent's work has funding/grant, I think that's ok since it's a work benefit such as healthcare.*

—CHARLES R.

*It disgusts me. It really shows how we, adoptees, are commodities to be purchased to the highest bidder.*

—LAUREN G.

*I do not support adoption fundraising by any means. Such funds [should] go to a mother in need of assistance supporting her child and mental health services so that she learns how to support her baby.*

—DANIELLE W.

*"Eh . . . iffy. I wouldn't donate to one.*

—AMANDA P.

*It feels icky. If you can't afford to adopt, don't do it. People fundraise to buy things, and one should not be buying a child.*

—DOUG E.

How was the experience of learning your birth culture's language? Did you ever feel embarrassed, angry, or judged? Please explain.

*It's been alright. Obviously, I'm not a pro at it, but I do pretty well. Chinese people who speak the language really well will say that my tones are not great or I need to improve. The comments make me a little insecure, but I get over it and use them as advice to improve.*

—RON W.

*I learned I was part Mexican when I was 13 and started studying it in high school. I do feel judged because I don't speak it properly. Not really accepted by any culture.*

—BILLY T.

*I've tried learning Spanish multiple times throughout my life. I was in Spanish class in middle school, and my Spanish teacher said something incredibly racist to me (he was white). I told the principal and my parents, and—shock, nobody believed me. I hated*

*Spanish after that, and studied Latin for five years in high school and college, a rather useless decision that hasn't helped me much with anything besides telling folks they're pronouncing their Latin-esque Harry Potter spells wrong.*

—HARRY S.

*Now, as an adult, when folks ask me if I'm Mexican, the follow-up question is always, "do you speak Spanish?" Which I don't. I've been made to feel that I am lesser—a person of color, sure, but not Latino. Just something else entirely.*

—DAVID D.

## How do you feel about adoption content in the media, like the Gerber Baby Announcement or adoption celebrations?

*Because of social media, we can see more adoptees' voices and various sources than before when it was controlled by media that catered to adoptive parents.*

—LILLIAN P.

*I think adoption celebrations are fine. I do think the media doesn't enlighten people enough on the negative impacts, mainly focuses on the positive.*

—GEORGE W.

*It depends on the story, but I overall abhor adoption celebration as it negates the trauma adoptees endure.*

—JULIA N.

## If you could give advice to a prospective adoptive parent, what would it be?

*Don't adopt; it's unnecessary. Help preserve a family. If you really have the best interest at heart for the child, you will do that.*

—FANNY C.

Do ALL your homework. Look into yourself and your family members and community to see if everyone is willing and has an open mind and [is] willing to be uncomfortable learning new things.

—TOM S.

It's not about you! It's about the child. For transracial adoption, be prepared to teach the child their culture, language, food, [and] traditions, [and] make friends with people from that culture as long as the child is willing and interested. If the child isn't interested at the time, always have the resources and connections available. I don't have too much for non-transracial besides the basics like listening to the child's needs, if possible, stay connected to the birth family, and don't speak badly about the birth family even if they haven't made the best life choices.

—BOB S.

Find a diverse place to live FIRST before adopting a child of color. Have friends of color—don't make your kid be one of the first people of color important to you. Don't live in a place where they'll feel isolated.

—KARA W.

Think long and hard about whether or not you are really equipped to adopt and are ready to change some things so that [your] children can grow up healthy.

—SAM P.

Why do you want to adopt? (Has to be a damn good reason.) Don't adopt a baby just because you're infertile. Spend at least one month in the child's birth country. [Ensure] that the child [has] any and all kinship connections intact. [Ensure] that the child has racial mirrors, positive role models, and sense of truth to their story as it is age-appropriate.

—PENNY B.

## ADOPTEE Q&A DISCUSSION GUIDE

As an adoptee, I know that reading through these questions and the various answers of transracial adoptees is apt to have been emotionally taxing. And I can imagine that it can be hard for adoptive parents and maybe a little discouraging. Just remember these responses were from a small survey of a fraction of adoptees. The opinions submitted were the answers of adoptees who were comfortable enough to express their opinions and lived experiences from a place of anonymity. I believe that many adoptees are content in their adoptive families, and there are those that simply weren't interested in filling out a survey about topics this personal. However, I find it incredibly refreshing that fifty adoptees *did* feel comfortable sharing bits of their stories to help adoptive parents who are willing to do the work. That said, please sit with the stories that these adoptees were willing to share because even if you do not believe your child feels the same, you can learn many lessons from their experiences.

Some of my biggest takeaways from these replies are that: 1) every adoptee's story is different; 2) transracial adoptees experience the world differently than our families do, and race/ethnicity has a big impact; and 3) adoption is complex, and some adoptees think that adoptive parents should do more work before and after adopting a child transracially.

Once you have read this section at least twice, please consider the following questions to help you create a list of your three most important takeaways:

- What surprised you?
- Did what you expected differ from what the adoptees wrote?
- How do you make sure your child is connected to their birth culture?
- Did any of the answers make you uncomfortable or defensive? And why?

- What do you think you're doing better than their white adoptive parents did?

- Could your child be experiencing similar problems?

- What are you currently doing to help your adopted child? What can you do better?

- If you asked your adopted child these questions, would they be completely honest with you?

- How can you improve your dialogue with your children?

# 8

## INTERVIEWS WITH ADOPTIVE PARENTS

Guilt. It's a constant theme for adoptees. We may feel guilty for being curious about our birth family, for asking our adoptive parents questions, or for struggling with our identities. As an adoptee, I wanted to discuss adoption openly with my parents, but often I was too afraid that they would get upset, or that their answers would hurt me.

Questioning white adoptive parents about their choices during their adoption processes can bring up their feelings about infertility, money anxiety, or even their concerns about not being "real-enough" parents. Often, even now, when I talk with my mother, we both get defensive when we should be listening to one another and validating each other's feelings. Because of the difficulties I have faced with discussing adoption, I thought it would be beneficial to ask white adoptive parents some questions that had been nagging me.

By keeping these surveys anonymous, I hoped to create a safe place for everyone to answer honestly about their experiences.

In the end, I was pleasantly surprised with the answers. Since I have received permission to share the responses anonymously, I am including some in this chapter.

## ———————————— ADOPTIVE PARENT SURVEY ————————————
## QUESTIONS AND ANONYMOUS ANSWERS

**Why did you choose international adoption?**

*We felt that our involvement in domestic networks needed to be more about reunification. We opted for an international program with a Hague country where the culture didn't allow for reunification opportunities.*

—C. N.

*Adoption agency recommended international due to our ages.*

—J. C.

**When did you begin to discuss race with your adopted child? And how do you discuss race/ethnicity?**

*We adopted her at just under 13 months old, and we always included her race and birth country in her story right away. At first, and for many years, we talked about China, and the things we saw there, read her Chinese stories, went to various activities for Chinese adoptees, etc. We started to notice that people referred to us as "the family with the Chinese daughter" in our small town and dealt with a few racists who were very rude to her and to us. We made the decision to move to an area with more Asian people so she could have friends who look like her.*

—K. S.

*She tells me she hates being black. I try to give good role models and tell her she's beautiful.*

—R. T.

*Only recently (within the past few years) have I realized that I need to talk about race. My child's racial background is largely unknown but assumed to be Italian, white, and African/African American based on physical appearance. We started by noticing and affirming similarities and differences in skin and eye color, noting the beauty in all people. I have begun to talk about racial issues and bias toward POC in the past year or so. I am aware that I will need to have better, deeper conversations with scarier topics, but I feel unsure of how to do that. I don't want to overwhelm my child, but I want to be truthful.*

—I. D.

## Does discussing racism/microaggressions make you nervous or uncomfortable? Please explain.

*Yes and no. I am nervous only because I don't have the first-hand experience with racism or being anything but white in America. But I acknowledge these issues still exist, and the best way to talk about it is openly and honestly with him.*

—B. M.

*Yes, it does, but I'm trying to get over that. I want to understand so I can learn to be better. And I want to confront friends and family members who do it both so they will learn but also so that my daughter will have the skills to confront and correct it. I was raised to be a "pleaser" and to not be "rude" to adults, [to] make peace. So, it has been hard for me to confront people about microaggressions and racism because I don't want to offend. But I am much better with it now because I don't want anyone hurting my daughter so that she feels less about herself. The hardest people to confront regarding racism and microaggressions are my in-laws because they don't believe they are doing it.*

—N. M.

*Sometimes I have to hold back from saying "not all white people," that is, feeling personally defensive when my daughter rails on "White people" for micro- or brutal racist aggression. She has the right, and she IS right, but I do feel uncomfortable and irritated.*

—E. C.

*I'd be lying if I said it doesn't. I feel like since I'm White, I've never experienced this first hand and am a little out of my depth. I recognize that native people in our community are discriminated against regularly, and it breaks my heart for what my daughter will inevitably experience as she grows. I'm doing my best to listen to the voices of POC and learn from what they're willing to share.*

—H. J.

## How old were your children when you told them they were adopted? How did you discuss it with them?

*I have pictures of their birth mom and birth sister in the house. We have many books talking about adoption; I mention it at least once a week. So . . . in theory, they will "always have known."*

—D. M.

*We talk about our adopted child's tummy mummy being different from the other two children.*

—H. L.

*She's always known. We have a picture book of happy pictures from the orphanage at home.*

—O. H.

*I made a book with my daughter's birth mom to give to her on her first birthday. The first few pages are written by her birth mom about why she chose us to be our daughter's parents. The rest of the book talks about the people in her family (adoptive and bio) and how they are related to her, and what they love to do with her.*

*We read this book to her often, and we have pictures of both her bio and adoptive family in her room and around our house. Long answer to say that there was never one moment or day that we revealed she was adopted.*

—P. C.

## Do you have an open adoption? If yes, how do you support the relationship?

*Yes. Currently, we text/share pictures with first family and occasionally FaceTime. We also share birthday/Christmas cards and gifts.*

—W. N.

*It's semi-open, so I write monthly—[and] at each of their "birthdays"—to the birth mom, sending photos, stories, etc.—but it goes through the Adoption Agency. In theory, she could write back (again, through the adoption agency), but as of now (23 months since I first adopted), she has not. I have the birth mom's full information—name, DOB, etc.—so Zola and Langston can find her when they're ready if we don't meet before then.*

—T. M.

*Tribal adoptions are not labeled "open" or "closed." We text or video chat with bio mom weekly. Her older daughters lived with us for a short time last year, and we were able to develop a relationship with them as well. We've helped bio mom out when she's asked by sending money, clothes, medicine, etc.*

—A. P.

*No. It's up to our child's birth family to determine if they'd like an open adoption or not. I hope this is something they choose in the future. We are still connected with our child's foster family.*

—O. B.

*No, her birth parents are not in the picture.*

—L. S.

## How do you integrate your child's birth culture?

*We both studied the language in high school, we'll visit the country often, we love the local food, the language will be studied in school, and we'll start celebrating public events and dress soon. I'd love to know the specific island his birth parents were from so we could localize that experience even more, and I'd love to be in touch with a member of his birth family to have more intimate conversations with them one day.*

—P. T.

*Cooking food from her culture, books, music, etc.—meetings with other people from her culture in the community.*

—J. R.

*I have a braiding teacher who I have studied with extensively. I take my daughter to her occasionally for the experience, even though I can braid myself now. We visit a Black-owned bookstore that has cultural programs throughout the year. We celebrate Kwanzaa at the bookstore and at home. We have sought out programs like Mocha Moms. We advocate at the public school for more Black History Month programming. We drive to the nearest city in the summer for programs at a majority-Black private school and dance school.*

—R. G-H.

*We live in the country he was born in. He has lessons in the language, all of the professionals in his life (teachers, doctors, etc. . .) look like him. We celebrate festivals, eat food. He has a passport from the country of his birth as well as my country.*

—E. B.

## How do you feel about adoption fundraising (aka raising money for adoption costs)?

*Totally fine with it and understand that it's necessary for some families.*

—D. M.

*I am very torn about it. We applied for a few grants for her adoption but raised almost all of it ourselves by working extra jobs and some family gifts. But fundraisers freak me out. Seems mercenary and icky. Our adoption was not a special needs adoption, and we weren't trying to "save" or "rescue" our daughter. I have given money to families who were adopting children with extreme special needs who seemed to be aging out of the care at their orphanages.*

—K. B.

*We don't agree with asking for money for adoption. Honestly, that same amount of money could go to help several families here make it through whatever struggle they're dealing with and keep their kids. And for some to just ask for it to be given? That being said, we did pick up extra jobs (some actual jobs, some more like cash jobs) to afford the whole process. We had garage sales. Occasionally friends who knew why we were doing all the extra stuff would donate something to the sale or tip on the box of cup-cakes they ordered from me to help us along.*

—M. C.

*We are in Australia, and it is not allowed. I agree with this rule.*

—I. W.

## What is the most difficult part of being an adoptive parent of a transracial adoptee?

*That I have SO much to learn and so far, to grow, to be a better resource for my African American child. It feels overwhelming—and (pity party!), I'm totally exhausted and sleep-deprived and deal with tantrums all day. I can't imagine "studying up" at the end of the day when they are both finally asleep! I feel pretty guilty about that.*

—F. V.

*Being a parent to a child. On the racial aspects, my only beef at the moment is people asking why one child looks different from the others. It feels like they're asking a parent of a child with dis-abilities "what's wrong with him?" and really, I feel like it's rude and none of their business.*

—K. P.

*I think the hardest part is realizing that I can't fix the hole in her heart that can only be filled by her biological family and birth culture. I can be the best mom possible and still not fix parts that are hurting. I can't save her from racism, and I can't help her feel really Chinese or really white.*

—N. B.

*Learning that I'm white. I always felt that being Jewish was a lot like being a POC but nope.*

—C. C.

*Being afraid of getting it wrong, of not being enough for him. I want him to be strong and confident in his identity.*

— T. S.

What is a mistake/awkward misstep you have made as an adoptive parent?

*There were a couple of times after the adoption, where I was a bit out of sorts, still trying to adjust to the new routine of things, where I answered with too much information to prying questions. Thankfully it was with trusted people and not incredibly sensitive* information, but I've been able to since go back and dialogue about the situation. Telling people that I won't answer a question was never a skill I felt like I needed to develop. I might not have ever thought about it at all. But we knew about it before the adoption, the protecting the story, that it's not ours to tell. I knew, and I've definitely gotten the practice in protecting it, but those first few times after cocooning, I was not prepared. There's definitely a difference between "knowing" something and "experiencing" something.

—E. R.

Probably taking trauma behaviors personally. Also, in the beginning, when we were all out as a multi-racial family, I probably answered too many questions from nosy people instead of just saying, "why do you ask?"

—P. O.

I seem to be more open to embracing and learning about customs from and history of their race than they are. I am learning to make the resources available to them but not to push it on them. Finding the balance is awkward and difficult to find and manage since it is fluid . . . through no fault of theirs.

—K. C.

## How do you feel when your child discusses their birth family?

Okay. I think I will always be a little sad that my child will never fully be mine, but I really want that birth family connection to happen someday for him to fill the gaps in his life. I would expect my child to care about his birth family and want to talk about them.

—N. S.

Happy to have an open dialogue. Happy, they get to know their mom. On occasion, jealous, but I try to push it back—I do NOT want my kids to censor their thoughts and feelings for my comfort, *and we make it a point to say on a regular basis that it is not their job to make adults feel comfortable. To speak their truth.*

—E. W.

*I'm usually fine, although she likes to bring it up when she's in trouble. It's an interesting place to be as a parent. Still steaming about whatever is then forced to do an about-face and be a good listener. I am not too good at calming down. She HATES getting in trouble, and I really believe that stems from abandonment. So, bringing up birth family makes sense! It's just really hard in reality, and something I could be better at.*

—R. G.

## How do you think you could have better prepared for being an adoptive parent of a transracial adoptee? What do you wish you would have known?

*I wish I were further along in my anti-racial journey. We've both been walking that path for a long time now, but it's only been these last few years for me of not working where I have the time to read and grow in a more current event sense. Working through the adoption process and then being a new mom puts you in survival mode, and you just put your head down and try to survive to the next day sometimes. Since coming out of that, I've been so thankful for all the new literature that's come out. A lot of good content and things that really help put words to systems, problems, etc. It's allowed us to be ready to frame it in a way our child will understand. If we had started more purposefully sooner, would anything have been different? Maybe? I would have felt more confident, I think, but I don't know what I would have changed yet.*

—D. M.

*Honestly, I do not think anyone could have told me anything! I thought I knew it all. But now I realize a part of me was in denial of difference or leaning toward a color-blind philosophy. Probably because I wanted it all to be easy. When my daughter first came, I lacked confidence, particularly about taking care of her hair. I had no clue and listened to random black people. I didn't understand that there were different cultural styles for textured hair . . . took her to a Haitian salon, then Afro-American. Let an Ethiopian friend chemically straighten her hair when she was five, got yelled at by African-American colleagues that I was going to give her brain cancer from the straightening, finally found a Senegalese braiding salon and went regularly there. I had no idea that time-consuming processes and infinite choices are the hair norm for black women. Wish I'd have known that!*

—S. N.

*I had my MSW when I adopted, specializing in child welfare, and I still wish I would have read more and talked more with adoptees. I wish I would have been told to let the small stuff go (i.e., grades don't mean shit if your child doesn't feel attached and bonded, so don't spend 3 hours a night working on homework) and focus most on building trust. Everything else will come if your child feels able to heal and trust with you. I wish I was told to carry that baby or kid as much as you can and slow down and snuggle and rock them more (even if they are 7 or 12).*

—G. C.

*So much, hair and skincare are huge, but we are getting the hang of it. Would be helpful to learn more about her culture and what would be some basics. Although we have many African American friends, we hate to have to ask everything.*

—V. N.

*wish again that I would have known that no one is entitled to her story, and I am not obligated to share it. Thankfully she is still very young, and we know now.*

—C. T.

*More training through our agency on the subject.*

—M. P.

*I mean, you can always prepare more, but I think role-playing question fielding would be the most helpful. I read A LOT of adoptee narratives and joined a few transracial adoptive groups, which helped (and continue to help) very, very much. I had the information I needed. I just needed the actual words and confidence to say them.*

—A. D.

## ADOPTIVE PARENT DISCUSSION GUIDE

When I put out a call to interview adoptive parents of transracial adoptees on Facebook, Twitter, and other various social media platforms, I did not expect to get the response that I did. Adoptive parents were jumping at the opportunity to help me, an adoptee, gather information to write a book about adoption. And overall, the answers were very honest and humble, surprising me further. I did not expect so many adoptive parents to be willing to own up to making mistakes along their adoption journey, and I certainly didn't expect them to let me include those responses in a book.

It was refreshing to see adoptive parents rally together and consider the fact that they may have made some blunders along the way. And, for me, this was the part of the experience that was the most powerful. So, as you read through this chapter, make sure to sit with each answer before considering what you could have done better than these other adoptive parents. Consider how you would parent going forward, if you were in their shoes. What do you think that adoptive parents can do now after admitting to certain mistakes?

I also encourage adoptive parents reading to answer each of the questions I posed to adoptive parents in this chapter, and then answer them again a few weeks or months later to track your progress. You may find it is beneficial to see how your attitudes and experiences have changed after parenting more mindfully.

# 9

# ACTIVITIES, RESOURCES, AND MORE

N o manual can prepare adoptive families for every hurdle they may face, but there are many and activities can definitely help. In this last chapter, I discuss some activities that will help adoptive parents incorporate more racial mirrors and coping skills while you work together with your entire family to make changes. This chapter helps point you in a more inclusive direction, from being mindful of the choices you make to the movies your family watches to the books you buy.

This chapter can supplement the material you read through earlier in this book to prepare you for the work you are now ready to do. Do not feel obligated to perform every activity and follow every direction word for word. These activities are adaptable to fit the needs of your family and adopted child(ren). Without further ado, here are a few tips, activities, and resources to help you work on your growth as an adoptive parent.

# ENCOURAGE INTERACTION IN ADOPTEE COMMUNITIES

As I began my journey toward acceptance and growth as an adoptee, I found that becoming involved in adoptee communities was one of the most helpful and influential parts. Unfortunately, I was not able to become involved in such communities until I was an adult because of when I found out I was adopted, but many other adoptees I have spoken with have reiterated to me that they felt great relief when they began becoming actively involved in adoption communities, no matter what age they were when they first began.

In an interview on my podcast, *Adoptee Thoughts*, Lauren J. Sharkey said this:

> *If I had access to that [adoptee] community at a younger age, . . . my life would've been exponentially different knowing there were other people struggling . . .*[1]

Since I began my podcast, I have gotten messages every week from adoptees thanking me for creating a place for them to share their stories and for them to hear the stories of other adoptees. When I get those messages, I feel relieved to have created such a safe place but also frustrated that adoptees have so few places in which they really feel seen. Often the stories I hear from adoptees, even those with "good" and happy relationships with their adoptive families, is that at the end of the day, they feel very isolated. Many did not have a strong support circle of fellow adoptees, and the few connections they did have were fleeting at best.

When you encourage your child to get out of their comfort zone and make connections with other adoptees, it can often open doors that they weren't aware of. Even if your children are grown, they can still benefit from such a suggestion.

I also urge you to gently encourage your children to find an adoptee community that they can be involved with in person or online, even if they brush you off the first few times. As children and even as adults, we often roll our eyes at suggestions our parents make, but this one has been very helpful to many adoptees. For example, often I have talked to adoptees whose parents put them in culture camps with other kids; it was only later that they realized how important those interactions were and how important having a circle of adoptees they could talk to was.

---

**Why is a support network of fellow adoptees so important?**

- Allows us to open up about questions and concerns we may be hesitant to share with our parents or non-adopted friends

- Validates many of our lived experiences[2]

- Increases our feeling of belonging and gives us a sense of community

- Often adds more racial mirrors of BIPOC that help us understand the adoptee experience

---

# FIND AN ADOPTION-COMPETENT THERAPIST OR MENTOR

When I sit down with a new therapist, I make sure to look for certain things. Some of the first questions I ask myself are these:

*Do I feel comfortable sharing my trauma with them?*

and . . .

*Do their comments ever make me feel judged?*

I like to think of finding a therapist as being like speed dating. You can narrow down your preferences ahead of time, but you're never quite sure what you're getting until you're face to face with the other person. For many people, finding the best therapist can be difficult, but adoptees have the added challenge of finding an adoption-competent therapist who is better prepared to address associated trauma. An adoption-competent therapist has completed accredited training in trauma-based adoption issues.[3] This allows them to connect with the adoptee and choose the most beneficial therapies.

One of the first therapists I saw encouraged me to cut ties with my adoptive family, the next one told me to be grateful, and at least three others seemed to be more uncomfortable than I was when I unloaded my complicated familial history. Finally, I was able to find a therapist who was adoption competent, and since then, I have made strides in creating boundaries with my family, reconciling my identity issues, and working on other mental health problems. Without an adoption-competent therapist, I know that I would not be at the place I am today.

When searching for an adoption-competent therapist, here are a few things to keep in mind.

### Qualities of an Adoption-Competent Therapist

- Will ask for a history prior to adoption
- Recognizes the importance of including family in the treatment plan
- Acknowledges loss as a core issue in adoption
- Is knowledgeable about the trauma rooted in adoption
- Is aware of the impact of attachment in mind and body

Three Great Websites to Search for an Adoption-
Competent Therapist

• https://adoptionsupport.org/member-types/adoption
  -competent-professionals/

• https://affcny.org/category/trauma-and-mental-health
  /adoption-competent-therapy/

• https://www.psychologytoday.com/us/therapists
  /adoption

# ENCOURAGE ACTIVITIES THAT FOSTER COPING SKILLS

Children, teenagers, and even adults can find it difficult to express themselves in a healthy way—particularly if they have had trauma. A study in 2016 found that adoptees are nearly twice as likely as non-adoptees to experience psychiatric disorders, to contact mental health services, or to be treated in a psychiatric hospital. It also found that adoptees have a continued elevated risk for attention deficit disorders, anxiety disorders, depression, substance use disorders, conduct or oppositional defiant disorders, and psychoses.[4]

Many adoptees may not be completely honest with our parents; we may be afraid of hurting their feelings or even feel guilty for thinking about our birth families. We may often feel like we're juggling on a seesaw and that we're one not-well-thought-out comment away from losing both of our families. When adoptees feel pressure to feel grateful, as well as a desire to connect with our birth family, it can lead to a lot of emotional turmoil.

In order to help adopted children learn how to express their feelings in a healthy way, adoptive parents can encourage them to engage in certain activities that allow them to express themselves. When we find a hobby that we love that allows us to express anger, jealousy, fear, or sadness without judgment, it can help our mental health. One study of at-risk youth found that engaging in a cultural arts program resulted in a significant reduction of mental health symptoms in females and behavior dysregulation in males.[5]

## Some Activities to Try

To encourage positive coping skills, here are a few activities for adoptees and a few for adoptive parents to work on. It's important to note that the younger the child, the more hands-on a parent may need to be. But as the adoptee matures, make sure to continue to be supportive, but also realize that it's okay for them to want some things to be private. In this case, encourage your child to share with a therapist or other trusted adult other than yourself.

### Writing Letters to a First Parent

Encourage your child to start compiling questions they have for their birth parent. Questions can be as simple as "What color are your eyes?" or more complex, like "Why did you place me for adoption?" No question is too silly or too personal in this activity. What is important is that your child has the freedom and support to feel safe enough to ask these questions in a controlled environment. I suggest purchasing a question box specifically for this purpose or even using a journal dedicated to this activity. No matter what, there is no wrong way to do this activity.

It is important for adoptive parents to encourage their children to engage in this activity while respecting their child's privacy. Do not pressure your child to share the letters and questions with you. This activity is aimed at making your child feel safe enough to express curiosity, love, and even anger toward their birth parents and having a safe place to do so.

### Producing Art of Any Kind

Making art can be therapeutic. Encourage your adopted child to express themselves in drawings, paintings, or even dance. Having a safe outlet in which to release their pent-up emotions can be a great stress reliever or can even function as a bridge they can use to begin communicating their feelings with a trusted adult.

### Becoming Active

In this case I'm not talking about physical exercise, although that kind of activity has many mental health benefits for the whole family. What I mean by *active* is this—become proactive when it comes to protecting your child from your friends', family's, and even strangers' inappropriate comments. Too often, I hear adoptees complain about awkward and even hostile environments that their adoptive parents could have helped prevent or at least could have shut down quickly so the adoptee would not have been subjected to intrusive questions or offensive language inadvertently.

For example, many transracial adoptees have heard the question "Is that your mom?" when they are out and about. And from a survey I conducted of many adoptive parents, the consensus was that they shared too much of their children's adoption stories—not just to family or friends, but to strangers as well.

In another case, an adoptive parent let their child be around racist family members.

*I have some family members who are racist. It has taken me a long time to realize that their actions, actions that I formerly just considered distasteful, are actually racist. I allowed them around my children for a very brief time. Then one day, I realized what I*

*was doing, and we have not been around that family since. That*
*was a hard decision, but I have to protect my children."*[6]

Thankfully, this adoptive parent realized the negative effects of letting their children be around the racist members of their family before the children were affected. In other cases, adoptees did not have parents who were so proactive. Sometimes adoptive parents denied their child's experience or made excuses for the person by saying it wasn't that serious. After all, most families have that old relative who is stuck in their ways.[7]

This is problematic. As a person with anxiety, I completely understand wanting to keep the peace and not create waves. But when people say racist things in front of you or to your children . . . even if they are family members, you *need* to shut that down, remove your child from that environment, and then, at a minimum, address the event with your child. When you become a parent of a child of color, it is your responsibility to protect them, even from "well-meaning" family members.

## Creating a Plan to Deal with Racism

Just as families prepare for fires in their home or for a natural disaster, adoptive families need to make a plan to deal with racism. A time will come when your child is exposed to racism by a beloved family member or family friend, and it is important to prepare for such an occasion before you think you need to.

Here are some questions to ask yourself:

- Am I willing to call out racist jokes?

- Am I willing to keep people who are unwilling to change out of my family's life?

- What would I say to a beloved family member who called my child a slur in public as a joke or even as a bad attempt at a compliment?

- How will I approach a situation in which my child comes up to me and says my sibling (their aunt) made fun of their eyes or performed some other microaggression?
- Am I willing to confront and shut down racism anywhere and immediately?
- Am I willing to do this in public? Or just at home?

When answering these questions, it's important to be honest with yourself, even if you have hesitations that you may be embarrassed to admit. Calling out racism is just like any other skill. It takes time and practice to perfect, and even when you are confident in yourself, you can stumble and end up in a painful and sometimes even awkward situation. What is important is that your children see that you will protect them, even from family members. These actions make a difference and will help prepare them for the future and teach them how to stand up to friends and family if they need to one day.

### Making Space on Birthdays and Holidays

A simple, yet effective, activity to help your adopted child during these special days is to make space for them emotionally and physically. Here are some quick-and-easy ways to make sure your child's birth family is included during special occasions.

- Set a spot at the dinner table for a birth mother or father to make a visual reminder for your child so the child knows the birth parent is loved and cherished in their family.
- Set aside wall space for pictures, letters, or mementos that remind your child of their birth family.
- Create a special playlist of traditional music from your child's birth culture.

These activities/actions are a great starting point from which you can make space for your child's birth family. In addition, taking steps like this can help guide your child to develop healthy coping mechanisms they can use to work through the complex emotions holidays may bring up. You can also schedule an extra therapy session for the holiday week or an extra hour or two of downtime so they have a safe place in which to unwind and simply feel what they need to feel. Encouraging self-expression and creating a safe place for your child can relieve some of the pressure many adoptees often face when they feel obligated to put on a happy and brave face during special occasions in order to protect their adoptive family's feelings.

## EASY ACTIVITIES FOR INCORPORATING RACIAL MIRRORS

Sometimes the most beneficial way to help children of color feel seen is by incorporating racial mirrors in their day-to-day lives. Consider adding some of the following movies, television shows, and books to your family's collection.

### Sharing the Spotlight

For every television show or movie you watch, make sure to include others that include racial mirrors of your child of color. Here are some suggestions:

**For Younger Children**

- *Dora the Explorer*
- *Go, Diego, Go*
- *Doc McStuffins*
- *Coco*
- *Moana*

- *BookMarks: Celebrating Black Voices*
- *Akeela and the Bee*
- *Spelling the Dream*
- *Raya and the Last Dragon*
- *Mira, Royal Detective*
- *Sophia the First*
- *Nella the Princess Knight*
- *Motown Magic*
- *Handy Manny*

### For Older Children

- *One Day at a Time*
- *Gente-fied*
- *Black Panther*
- *Jane the Virgin*
- *To All the Boys I Loved Before*
- *All Together Now*
- *Hidden Figures*
- *The Hate U Give*
- *Black-ish*
- *Fresh Off the Boat*
- *Spider-Man: Into the Spider-Verse*
- *A Ballerina's Tale*

## Decolonizing Your Bookshelf

Take inventory of all of the literature in your home and tally how many books are by white, Black, Indigenous, and other persons of color. If you find that more than half of your books are by white authors, now is a great time to purchase new books by more #ownvoice authors. #Ownvoice books are written by people from marginalized groups about their own experiences/perspectives.

## Embracing Diverse Activities

It is easy to fall into a routine with your family of being involved in the same after-school activities. After all, some may be provided by your school or church, which can make it a breeze to sign up. But it is important to join activities that allow your child to be a part of a more diverse group. Instead of just cheerleading or sports activities, try to find local dance groups or martial arts groups or other cultural groups that will allow your child to expand their engagement with a community of people who look like them.

## Need a Mirror?

I challenge all adoptive families to list three or four big occasions that you celebrate with friends or family. Next, list all the friends and family that you typically see during family barbeques or birthday parties. Once you have a list of names, highlight all of the names of people whose racial identity is white, next circle people of color. How many racial mirrors do your children have? If they are grossly outnumbered during the majority of holidays, birthday celebrations, and even neighborhood potlucks, it is time to work on diversifying your circles.

# RESOURCES

Here are a few lists of books and online resources for kids and adults about adoption and race.

NOTE  *Denotes books written by adoptees.

## Books for Kids

- *All Kinds of Families*, by Suzanne Lang
- *And Tango Makes Three*, by Justin Richardson and Peter Parnell
- *And That's Why She's My Mama*, by Tiarra Nazario
- *Coco & Olive: The Color of Love*, by Michelle Madrid-Branch*
- *The Family Book*, by Todd Parr
- *A Mother for Choco*, by Keiko Kasza
- *Stellaluna*, by Janell Cannon

## Books about Adoption

- *Adoption Healing*, by Joe Soll*
- *All You Can Ever Know: A Memoir*, by Nicole Chung*
- *American Baby: A Mother, a Child, and the Shadow History of Adoption*, by Gabrielle Glaser
- *The Baby Scoop Era: Unwed Mothers, Infant Adoption, and Forced Surrender*, by Karen Wilson-Buterbaugh*
- *Bitterroot: A Salish Memoir of Transracial Adoption*, by Susan Devan Harness*
- *Famous Adopted People*, by Alice Stephens*
- *For Black Girls Like Me*, by Mariama J. Lockington*
- *The Girls Who Went Away: The Hidden History of Women Who Surrendered Children for Adoption in the Decades Before Roe v. Wade*, by Ann Fessler*
- *Growing Up Black in White*, by Kevin D. Hofmann*
- *Inconvenient Daughter*, by Lauren J. Sharkey*

- *In Their Voices: Black Americans on Transracial Adoption*, by Rhonda M. Roorda*
- *The Lived Experiences of Colombian Adoptees*, edited by Abby Forero-Hilty*
- *A Long Way Home: A Memoir*, by Saroo Brierley*
- *Lucky Girl*, by Mei-Ling Hopgood*
- *Motherhood So White: A Memoir of Race, Gender, and Parenting in America*, by Nefertiti Austin
- *Not My White Savior: A Memoir in Poems*, by Julayane Lee*
- *Older Sister. Not Necessarily Related: A Memoir*, by Jenny Heijun Wills*
- *Palimpsest: Documents from a Korean Adoption*, by Lisa Wool-Rim Sjöblom*
- *The Primal Wound*, by Nancy Newton Verrier
- *A Princess Found: An American Family, an African Chiefdom, and the Daughter Who Connected Them All*, by Sarah Culberson* and Tracy Trivas
- *Searching for Mom: A Memoir*, by Sara Easterly*
- *See No Color*, by Shannon Gibney*
- *Selling Transracial Adoption: Families, Markets, and the Color Line*, by Elizabeth Raleigh*
- *Set Free: A Childhood Memoir*, by Destini McAlister*
- *Surviving the White Gaze: A Memoir*, by Rebecca Carroll*
- *Through Adopted Eyes: A Collection of Memoirs from Adoptees*, by Elena S. Hall*
- *Welcome Home: An Anthology on Love and Adoption*, by Eric Smith*

## Diverse Books for Kids

- *Alma and How She Got Her Name,* by Juana Martinez-Neal
- *Bad Hair Does Not Exist!,* by Sulma Arzu-Brown
- *The Colors of Us,* by Karen Katz
- *Dreamers,* by Yuyi Morales
- *From North to South,* by René Colato Laínez
- *Happy in Our Skin,* by Fran Manushkin
- *I Am Enough,* by Grace Byers
- *Islandborn,* by Junot Díaz
- *Little Legends: Bold Women in Black History,* by Vashti Harrison
- *Love Makes a Family,* by Sophie Beer
- *Sulwe,* by Lupita Nyong'o
- *Think Big, Little One,* by Vashti Harrison

## Books on Anti-Racism

- *Between the World and Me,* by Ta-Nehisi Coates
- *The Color of Law: A Forgotten History of How Our Government Segregated America,* by Richard Rothstein
- *How to Be an Antiracist,* by Ibram X. Kendi
- *Inventing Latinos: A New Story of American Racism,* by Laura E. Gómez
- *Just Mercy: A Story of Justice and Redemption,* by Bryan Stevenson
- *Me and White Supremacy,* by Layla F. Saad
- *The New Jim Crow: Mass Incarceration in the Age of Colorblindness,* by Michelle Alexander

- *Racism without Racists: Color-Blind Racism and the Persistence of Racial Inequality*, by Eduardo Bonilla-Silva

- *Raising White Kids: Bringing Up Children in a Racially Unjust America*, by Jennifer Harvey

- *So You Want to Talk About Race*, by Ijeoma Oluo

## Instagram Pages focused on Transracial Adoption

- @adoptee_thoughts by Melissa Guida-Richards
- @fereraswan by Ferera Swan
- @hannahjacksonmatthews by Hannah Matthews
- @iamadopted by Jessenia Parmer
- @isaac_etter by Isaac Etter
- @katiethekad by Katie Baird
- @patrickintheworld by Patrick Armstrong
- @theljsharks by Lauren J Sharkey
- @therapyredeemed by Cam Lee Small, MS (*Adoption-informed therapist*)
- @thisadopteelife by Amanda
- @wreckageandwonder by Torie DiMartile

## Podcasts

- *Adopted Feels* by Hana and Ryan
- *Adoptees On* by Haley Radke
- *The Adoptee Next Door* by Angela Tucker
- *Adoptee Thoughts* by Melissa Guida-Richards
- *Adoption Advocacy Podcast* by Ryan Frisbie

- *Adoption Now* by April Fallon
- *The Janchi Show* by Patrick Armstrong, Nathan Nowack, and K. J. Roelke
- *When They Were Young: Amplifying Voices of Adoptees* by Lanise Antoine Shelley

**Websites**

- Adoptee Bridge: https://adopteebridge.org
- AdopteeLit: https://adopteelit.com
- Adoptive and Foster Family Coalition: https://affcny.org
- Adoption Mosaic: http://www.adoptionmosaic.org
- Embrace Race: https://www.embracerace.org/resources/topic/transracial-adoption
- Etter Consulting: https://isaacetter.com
- Intercountry Adoptee Voices: https://intercountryadopteevoices.com
- Plan A Magazine: https://planamag.com/adoption/

**YouTube Channel**

- LillyFei: https://www.youtube.com/channel/UCCDR80SruJ6QyGJzvX5CmcA

**Facebook Groups**

- Adopted From Colombia: https://www.facebook.com/groups/300252376782700
- Intercountry Adoptee Voices (ICAV): https://www.facebook.com/groups/Intercountryadopteevoices

- Transracial Adoption: https://www.facebook.com /groups/TransracialAdoption
- Transracial Adoption—Community of Learning and Support: https://www.facebook.com/groups /626044057491297
- Transracial Adoption Perspectives: https://www .facebook.com/groups/transracialperspectives

## Documentaries

- *Black, White & US*, directed by Loki Mulholland, January 2019
- *Calcutta Is My Mother*, directed by Reshma McClintock, January 2019
- *Closure*, directed by Bryan Tucker, December 2013
- *Lion*, directed by Saroo Brierley, October 2016
- *Outside Looking In: Transracial Adoption in America*, directed by Phil Bertelsen, November 2008
- *Passing Through*, directed by Nathan Adolfson, 1999
- *Side by Side*, directed by Glenn Morey and Julie Morey, May 2018

## Essays by Adoptees

- Nicole Chung, "Stories of Transracial Adoptees Must Be Heard—Even Uncomfortable Ones," https://www .theguardian.com/commentisfree/2019/apr/04/ transracial-adoption-listen-understand
- Stephanie Drenka, "I'm Adopted and Pro-Choice. Stop Using My Story for the Anti-Abortion Agenda,"

https://www.huffpost.com/entry/adopted-and-pro
-choice_n_5ced7bfde4b0356205a0a5c4

• ———, "I'm Adopted, But I Won't Be Celebrating
National Adoption Month," https://www.huffpost.com
/entry/national-adoption-awareness-month-adoptee
-perspective_n_5b3b9f5de4b09e4a8b27e53b

• Hannah Grieco, "Finding the Missing Piece: What
Happens When Adoptees Become Parents," https://
www.washingtonpost.com/lifestyle/2020/05/01
/finding-missing-piece-what-happens-when-adoptees
-become-parents/

• ———, "A Bridge between Adoptive and Birth Families," https://www.thecut.com/2019/01/nicole-chung
-what-is-a-family.html

• Melissa Guida-Richards, "Abby Johnson's Video
Shows the Problem with White Parents Adopting
Children of Color," https://zora.medium.com/abby
-johnsons-video-shows-the-problem-with-white
-parents-adopting-children-of-color-949b602e1328

• ———, "My Half Siblings Found Me on 23andMe. I
Wasn't Prepared for What Happened Next," https://
www.huffpost.com/entry/discovered-siblings-reunited
-23andme-dna-test_n_5e690e55c5b60557280f743e

• ———, "I Was Adopted Outside of the US and Have
Disabilities. I'm Tired of the Savior Narrative Among
White Adoptive Parents," https://www.insider.com
/im-an-adoptee-im-tired-white-saviors-like-myka
-stauffer-2020-6#:~:text=I%20was%20adopted%20
outside%20of,narrative%20among%20white%20
adoptive%20parents.&text=When%20Melissa%20

Guida%2DRichards%20learned,autism%2C%20
the%20writer%20was%20distraught.

- ———, "My Adoptive Parents Hid My Racial Identity from Me for 19 Years," https://www.huffpost
  .com/entry/transracial-adoption-racial-identity_n
  _5c94f7eae4b01ebeef0e76e6

- ———, "How Immersion into My Own Food
  Culture Changed Me as an Adoptee," https://zora
  .medium.com/how-immersion-into-my-own-food
  -culture-changed-me-as-an-adoptee-460504552fe

- Steve Haruch, "Why I Stopped Celebrating My
  'Birthday,'" https://catapult.co/stories/steve-haruch
  -adopted-series-why-i-stopped-celebrating-my
  -birthday

- Tony Hynes, "Why We Shouldn't Call Adoptees
  'Lucky,'" https://catapult.co/stories/essay-adopted
  -why-we-shouldnt-call-adoptees-lucky-tony-hynes#:
  ~:text=When%20we%20insinuate%20that%20
  an,as%20any%20parent%20can%20be

- Spencer Lee Lenfield, "Korean as a Second Language," https://catapult.co/stories/adopted-korean
  -as-a-second-language

- Mariama J. Lockington, "What a Black Woman
  Wishes Her Adoptive White Parents Knew," https://
  www.buzzfeednews.com/article/mariamalockington
  /what-a-black-woman-wishes-her-adoptive-white
  -parents-knew

- Joy Lieberthal Rho, "One Mother, Two Mothers, No
  Mother," https://catapult.co/stories/adopted-essay
  -when-adoption-isnt-forever-joy-lieberthal-rho

# TERMINOLOGY

Marietta Spencer introduced the adoption community to a new set of adoption language that uses primarily positive terminology.[8] She advocated leaving behind words like *abandoned* and *real parents* in favor of terms like *placed* and *birth mother*. Spencer thought that using positive language would empower people in the adoption and foster care community while also fighting stereotypes of adoption. This practice is often referred to as *positive adoption language (PAL)* or *respectful adoption language (RAL)*.

When we discuss terminology, it is easy to fall into a cookie-cutter viewpoint of adoption by adhering to primarily PAL or RAL. In a paper, Karen Wilson-Buterbaugh critiques the use and advocation of PAL and states that when we use this language, it can hide the inconvenient truths of adoption by whitewashing, when in fact, certain adoption practices should be held to a higher standard.[9] She also argues that using this language dismisses the experiences of many who have been affected by the industry.

When you think about the language used in the adoption community versus the language made by others outside of the adoption community, there is often a disconnect. A recent thread on Twitter asked adoptees, "Which adoption term are you most triggered by and want to see it gone?"[10] Adoptees included many of the following terms or phrases.

Common language/terms:

- Gotcha day
- Forever family
- Placed for adoption
- Adoption triad

- Birth mom
- Orphan
- Relinquished
- Better life
- *Adopted* children (as a qualifier used in death announcements, rather than just referring to the kids as children)
- Lost to adoption
- Adoption plan
- Rehoming
- Adoption disruption
- Sibling contact
- Family of origin
- Natural parent

**Phrases adoptive parents have used:**
- Called to adopt
- God spoke to us
- Born in my heart
- "She *loved* you so much; she gave you away."
- We were called to adopt
- We don't see color
- Tummy mommy
- Transracial adoption is a "teachable moment" for friends, family, etc.
- "You get this from me," speaking as if adoptees share adoptive parents' DNA

**Language used by those outside the adoption triad:**

- Referring to adoptees as being "rescued," "saved," "lucky," "ungrateful," "chosen," "bitter," or "angry"
- Referring to birth parents as "your real Mom/Dad"
- Saying things like "Your story is inspiring"
- Referring to adoption as "paper pregnancy"
- Claiming women with unwanted pregnancies should "just give the child up for adoption"
- Referring to an adoptive family's biological children as the adoptive parents' "own" children

Adoptive parents often advocate for people to use positive adoption language, and I urge you to question *why* adoptive parents and prospective adoptive parents feel more comfortable using it. Why are they more comfortable framing the narrative with phrases that often sugar coat what many adoptees feel happened? Often as an adoptee, I feel abandoned, given up. My thoughts toward my adoption are complicated at best, and every time I see an adoptive parent "correct" an adoptee online for using more realistic language, it is frustrating. This tone policing is exhausting and frustrating, and it silences the voices of the most fragile group in the adoption community.

As adoptees, we need support and honest language when it comes to discussing adoption experiences. We will never have perfect terminology that doesn't offend anyone, but there are better options depending on who you are talking to in the community. Adoptive parents and even birth parents will have language that they prefer because it makes them feel better, but adoptees tend to prefer language that suits the nuanced emotions adoption triggers in them. And the truth is that there is no one-size-fits-all language. When adoptive parents ask what language is best, I cannot give a good answer . . . because there isn't one. What works for one adoptee may not work for another. But what many adoptees agree on is that we do not appreciate or care for positive adoption language. We find it offensive.

One parent I spoke with anonymously shared the following learning experience.

*In the first few weeks, my legacy language was still there. I'd refer to my biological kids as my kids and imply my third child wasn't mine. I felt terrible. My middle child did the same sort of thing, saying "don't hurt my brother," but now she would say, "don't hurt your big brother," that sort of thing.*[11]

Remember that you will make mistakes along the road. It happens. What is important is that you are able to acknowledge your missteps and learn from those experiences. Make sure you are validating your child's feelings and respecting their preferences as to what type of language they prefer. Do not fall back on excuses and nicknames that you personally prefer because you find them cute. Do not use terms such as *Coconut* or describe their skin color using foods, because they can often be microaggressions.

You will find some terms more favorable; just remember, an adoptee should be able to reserve the right to correct you at any point and ask you to refrain from using certain language in conversations. Certain words and phrases can be very triggering to hear, so it is important to support adoptees instead of arguing with them and rejecting their opinion because you don't agree with it. Of the almost one hundred different comments by adoptees who answered a quick poll on Twitter, most seemed to show similar distaste for positive adoption language.[12] To get you started, here are a few of the terms and phrases I personally use.

Honest adoption language often preferred by adoptees:

- Refer to birth parents as First Mom, First Dad, or simple "Mother" or "Father."
- Do not say it was "God's Plan" or things to that effect.
- Engage in honest discussions of the adoptee's adoption story that are age-appropriate.
- Don't refer to a child being adopted as being "surrendered for adoption" or similar language.

## THE ADOPTIVE PARENT PROMISE

As an adoptive parent, I understand that it is my responsibility to learn about and foster ethical adoption practices. I promise to develop and maintain cultural competency so I can teach my children about their race/ethnicity, language, and the traditions of their birth culture. I promise to actively listen to my adopted child and value their opinion as well as the voices of adults who were adopted.

I promise to celebrate my child's race/culture and never let colorblindness cloud my vision. I promise to call out the racism and microaggressions of my friends and family members and protect my child. I promise to believe my child when they tell me they have experienced racism and to support them in any way I can.

I am aware that adoption is multifaceted and that I am coming from a place of privilege that can make it hard to fully empathize with adoptees. Therefore, I promise to do my best by learning more, by asking questions, and by apologizing when I make mistakes. I will support my child no matter how they feel about adoption and will engage in an open dialogue, even if I feel defensive. I promise to respect *their* story and only share what my child is comfortable with me telling others online and in person.

Above all, I promise to love my child and never make them feel like they are ungrateful.

## BILL OF RIGHTS FOR TRANSRACIAL ADOPTEES

I have the right...

- To express my feelings about adoption in any way I see fit.
- To identify with all of the cultures in my life—birth and adoptive.
- To grow and evolve my identity over time.
- To not have to justify who my family is.
- To have access to my birth certificate.
- To engage and be around my birth family as long as it is safe to do so.
- To refuse to engage with my birth family if I am not ready.
- To have any feelings toward my birth parents that make sense to me.
- To love my adoptive parents and birth parents.
- To be angry with the system of adoption.
- To talk about adoption without being seen as an ungrateful adoptee.
- To share my adoption story as I see fit.
- Not to be seen as a charity case.
- To love and identify with different parts of my family and culture.
- To feel differently than other adoptees.

For people to respect *my* story.

# NOTES

## Preface

1 Leslie Hollingsworth and Verlie Mae Ruffm, "Why Are So Many U.S. Families Adopting Internationally?" *Journal of Human Behavior in the Social Environment* 6, no. 1 (2002): 81–97, https://doi.org /10.1300/J137v06n01_06.

2 Rachel Garlinghouse, "In Today's America, My Black Son Is in Danger," Scary Mommy, May 30, 2020, https://www.scarymommy .com/raising-black-son-the-talk/.

3 Akilah Dulin-Keita, Lonnie Hannon III, Jose R. Fernandez, and William C. Cockerham, "The Defining Moment: Children's Conceptualization of Race and Experiences with Racial Discrimination," *Ethnic and Racial Studies* 34, no. 4 (2011): 662–682, https://doi.org/10.108 0/01419870.2011.535906.

4 Jessica Sullivan, Evan P. Apfelbaum, and Leigh Wilton, "Children Notice Race Several Years Before Adults Want to Talk About It," August 27, 2020, https://www.apa.org/news/press/releases/2020/08 /children-notice-race, from Jessica Sullivan, Leigh Wilton, and Evan P. Apfelbaum, "Adults Delay Conversations about Race Because They Underestimate Children's Processing of Race," *Journal of Experimental Psychology: General*, August 6, 2020.

5 Margaret A. Keyes, Stephen M. Malone, Anu Sharma, William G. Iacono, and Matt McGue, "Risk of Suicide Attempt in Adopted and Nonadopted Offspring," *Pediatrics* 132, no. 4 (2013): 639–46, https://doi.org/10.1542/peds.2012-3251.

6  Anders Hjern, Frank Lindblad, and Bo Vinnerljung, "Suicide, Psychiatric Illness, and Social Maladjustment in Intercountry Adoptees in Sweden: A Cohort Study," *The Lancet* 360, no. 9331 (2002): 443–48, https://doi.org/10.1016/S0140-6736(02)09674-5.
7  Madeline H. Engel, Norma K. Phillips, and Frances A. Della Cava, "Inter-Country Adoption of Children Born in the United States," *Sociology Between the Gaps: Forgotten and Neglected Topics Volume 1*, Providence.edu (Fall 2014–Summer 2015), https://digitalcommons.providence.edu/cgi/viewcontent.cgi?article=1000&context=sbg.
8  Melea VanOstrand, "'I'm Not Racist. I Have a Black Family Member!' I'm That Black Family Member. Yes, You Are Racist," Medium, August 13, 2020, https://medium.com/@meleavanostrand/im-not-racist-i-have-a-black-family-member-i-m-that-black-family-member-yes-you-are-racist-ba08b0d1e50d.

## Introduction

1  Rose M. Kreider and Daphne A. Lofquist, "Adopted Children and Stepchildren: 2010," *Current Population Reports*, US Census Bureau, P20-572 (Washington, DC: U.S. Department of Commerce, 2014).
2  Elisha Marr, "US Transracial Adoption Trends in the 21st Century." *Adoption Quarterly* 20, no. 3 (April 3, 2017): 222–51, https://doi.org/10.1080/10926755.2017.1291458.

## Chapter 1

1  Judith Penny, DiAnne Borders, and Francie Portnoy, "Reconstruction of Adoption Issues: Delineation of Five Phases Among Adult Adoptees," *Journal of Counseling and Development* 85, no. 1 (2007): 30–41, https://adopta.hr/images/pdf/reconstruction_of_adoption_issues.pdf.
2  Penny, Borders, and Portnoy, "Reconstruction of Adoption Issues."
3  Melea VanOstrand, "'I'm Not Racist. I Have a Black Family Member!' 'I'm That Black Family Member. Yes, You Are Racist." Medium, August 13, 2020, https://medium.com/@meleavanostrand/im-not-racist-i-have-a-black-family-member-i-m-that-black-family-member-yes-you-are-racist-ba08b0d1e50d.

4  VanOstrand, "I'm Not Racist."

5  Teju Cole, "The White-Savior Industrial Complex," *The Atlantic*, March 20, 2012, https://www.theatlantic.com/international /archive/2012/03/the-white-savior-industrial-complex/254843/.

6  Teju Cole (@tejucole), Twitter thread, March 8, 2012, https://twitter .com/tejucole/status/177809396070498304?s=20.

7  Alison Bowman, Laura Hofer, Collin O'Rourke, and Lindsay Read, *Racial Disproportionality in Wisconsin's Child Welfare System* (Madison, WI: Robert M. La Follette School of Public Affairs, University of Wisconsin-Madison, May 12, 2009), https://lafollette.wisc .edu/images/publications/workshops/2009-racial.pdf.

8  Anonymous survey for adoptive parents, conducted and created by author on May 20, 2020, https://docs.google.com/forms/d/1G7tKf J3TZP86r90n36T2Q7XpF9ooWftMVRv8p4AQ1CQ/edit.

9  Jessica Davis, "The 'Orphan' I Adopted from Uganda Already Had a Family," CNN, October 14, 2017, https://www.cnn.com/2017/10/13 /opinions/adoption-uganda-opinion-davis.

10  Davis, "'Orphan' I Adopted Had a Family."

11  Corinna Csáky, *Keeping Children Out of Harmful Institutions: Why We Should Be Investing in Family-Based Care* (London: Save the Children, 2009), http://www.thinkchildsafe.org/thinkbeforedonating /wp-content/uploads/Keeping-Children-Out-of-Harmful-Institutions -Save-The-Children.pdf.

12  Sarah Rahal, "Agency's Move to Stop Foreign Adoptions Leaves Few Options in Michigan," *The Detroit News*, February 13, 2020, https://www.detroitnews.com/story/news/local/michigan/2020/02/12 /agencys-move-bar-foreign-adoptions-leaves-few-options-michigan /4654654002/.

13  Rahal, "Agency's Move Leaves Few Options."

14  Associated Press, "Read Amy Coney Barrett's Full Prepared Opening Statement for Supreme Court Hearing," PBS News Hour/Nation: PBS.org, October 12, 2020, https://www.pbs.org/newshour/nation /read-amy-coney-barretts-full-prepared-opening-statement-for -supreme-court-hearing.

15  Associated Press, "Read Barrett's Opening Statement."

16  Graig Graziosi, "Amy Coney Barrett Ruled Using the n-Word Does Not Make a Work Environment Hostile," *The Independent*, October

15, 2020, https://www.independent.co.uk/news/world/americas/us
-politics/amy-coney-barrett-confirmation-supreme-court-n-word
-b1016358.html.

17  Melissa Guida-Richards, "My Adoptive Parents Hid My Racial
Identity from Me for 19 Years," February 11, 2021, https://www
.huffpost.com/entry/transracial-adoption-racial-identity_n_5c94f7
eae4b01ebeef0e76e6.

18  Mariama Lockington, "What a Black Woman Wishes Her Adoptive
White Parents Knew," *BuzzFeed News*, August 5, 2016, https://
www.buzzfeednews.com/article/mariamalockington/what-a-black
-woman-wishes-her-adoptive-white-parents-knew.

19  Nicole Chung, "People Want to Hear That I'm Happy I Was
Adopted. It's Not That Simple," *BuzzFeed News*, November 15,
2020, https://www.buzzfeednews.com/article/nicolechung/being
-korean-and-adopted-by-white-parents-nicole-chung.

20  Melissa Guida-Richards, "Abby Johnson's Video Shows the Problem
with White Parents Adopting Children of Color," ZORA, Medium,
August 28, 2020, https://zora.medium.com/abby-johnsons-video
-shows-the-problem-with-white-parents-adopting-children-of-color
-949b602e1328.

21  Dena@Write-Solutions, comment on Guida-Richards, "Abby Johnson's Video Shows the Problem."

# Chapter 2

1  Konstantin Lukin, "Toxic Positivity: Don't Always Look on the
Bright Side," *Psychology Today*, August 1, 2019, https://www
.psychologytoday.com/us/blog/the-man-cave/201908/toxic-positivity
-dont-always-look-the-bright-side.

2  Oxford Academic, "Understanding Adoption: A Developmental
Approach," *Paediatrics and Child Health* 6, no. 5 (2001): 281–91.
https://doi.org/10.1093/pch/6.5.281.

3  Stefano Vaglio, "Chemical Communication and Mother-Infant Recognition," *Communicative and Integrative Biology* 2, no. 3 (2009):
279–81, https://doi.org/10.4161/cib.2.3.8227.

4  Lee Dye, "Babies Recognize Mom's Voice from the Womb," ABC News,
January 7, 2006, https://abcnews.go.com/Technology/story?id=97635.

5  Nancy Newton Verrier, *The Primal Wound* (Baltimore: Gateway, 2012).

6  Oxford Academic, "Understanding Adoption," 281–83.

7  Hurley Riley, "The Impact of Parent-Child Separation at the Border," University of Michigan School of Public Health, September 7, 2018, https://sph.umich.edu/pursuit/2018posts/family-separation-US-border.html.

8  Margaret A Keyes, Stephen M. Malone, Anu Sharma, William G. Iacono, and Matt McGue, "Risk of Suicide Attempt in Adopted and Nonadopted Offspring," *Pediatrics* 132, no. 4 (2013): 639–46, https://doi.org/10.1542/peds.2012-3251.

9  Ann E. Bigelow, Michelle Power, Kim MacLean, Doris Gillis, Michelle Ward, Carolyn Taylor, Lindsay Berrigan, and Xu Wang, "Mother–Infant Skin-to-Skin Contact and Mother–Child Interaction 9 Years Later," *Social Development* 27, no. 4 (June 16, 2018): 937–51, https://doi.org/10.1111/sode.12307.

10  Janet Anormaliza, Facebook photo and caption, June 21, 2020, https://www.facebook.com/photo.php?fbid=10156925140466879&set=p.10156925140466879&type=3&theater.

11  Richard M. Lee, "The Transracial Adoption Paradox: History, Research, and Counseling Implications of Cultural Socialization," *The Counseling Psychologist* 31, no. 6 (November 1, 2003): 711–44, https://doi.org/10.1177/0011000003258087.

12  Candice Presseau, Cirleen DeBlaere, and Linh P. Luu, "Discrimination and Mental Health in Adult Transracial Adoptees: Can Parents Foster Preparedness?" *American Journal of Orthopsychiatry* 89, no. 2 (2019): 192–200, https://doi.org/10.1037/ort0000385.

13  Sydney K. Morgan and Kimberly J. Langrehr, "Transracially Adoptive Parents' Colorblindness and Discrimination Recognition: Adoption Stigma as Moderator." *Cultural Diversity and Ethnic Minority Psychology* 25, no. 2 (2019): 242–52, https://doi.org/10.1037/cdp0000219.

14  Kevin L. Nadal, Katie E. Griffin, Yinglee Wong, Sahran Hamit, and Morgan Rasmus, "The Impact of Racial Microaggressions on Mental Health: Counseling Implications for Clients of Color," *Journal of Counseling and Development* 92, no. 1 (2014): 57–66, https://doi.org/10.1002/j.1556-6676.2014.00130.x.

15 Nadal et al., "Impact of Racial Microaggressions on Mental Health," 57–66.

16 Nadal et al., "Impact of Racial Microaggressions on Mental Health," 57–66.

17 Nadal et al., "Impact of Racial Microaggressions on Mental Health," 57–66.

18 Sumie Okazaki, "Impact of Racism on Ethnic Minority Mental Health," *Perspectives on Psychological Science* 4, no. 1 (January 2009): 103–07, Accessed December 10, 2020, http://www.jstor.org /stable/40212301.

19 Elena Rivera, "Lack of Therapists of Color Creates Barriers to Mental Health Access," WFAE 90.7: Charlotte's NPR News Source, July 24, 2019, https://www.wfae.org/local-news/2019-07-24/lack-of -therapists-of-color-creates-barriers-to-mental-health-access.

20 Rivera, "Lack of Therapists of. Color."

21 Rivera, "Lack of Therapists of Color."

22 Kimberly J. Langrehr, Sydney K. Morgan, Jessica Ross, Monica Oh, and Wen Wen Chong, "Racist Experiences, Openness to Discussing Racism, and Attitudes toward Ethnic Heritage Activities: Adoptee– Parent Discrepancies," *Asian American Journal of Psychology* 10, no. 2 (2019): 91–102, https://doi.org/10.1037/aap0000128.supp (Supplemental).

23 Darron T. Smith, Brenda G. Juarez, and Cardell K. Jacobson, "White on Black: Can White Parents Teach Black Adoptive Children How to Understand and Cope with Racism?" *Journal of Black Studies* 42, no. 8 (November 2011): 1195–230, Accessed December 9, 2020, http://www.jstor.org/stable/41304581.

24 Langrehr et al., "Racist Experiences."

25 Kristen Pauker, Amanda Williams, and Jennifer Steele, "Children's Racial Categorization in Context," *Child Development Perspectives* 10, no. 1 (March 2016): 33–38, https://doi.org/10.1111/cdep .12155.

26 H. A. Neville, M. E. Gallardo, and D. W. Sue, "Introduction: Has the United States Really Moved Beyond Race?" in H.A. Neville, M.E. Gallardo, and D.W. Sue (eds), *The Myth of Racial Color Blindness: Manifestations, Dynamics, and Impact* (American Psychological Association, 2016), 3–21, https://doi.org/10.1037/14754-001.

27 John Gramlich, "The Gap between the Number of Blacks and Whites in Prison Is Shrinking," Pew Research Center, Factank, News in the Numbers, April 30, 2019, https://www.pewresearch.org/fact-tank/2019/04/30/shrinking-gap-between-number-of-blacks-and-whites-in-prison/.

28 Neville, Gallardo, and Sue, "Has the United States Really Moved Beyond Race?"

29 Richard M. Lee, Harold D. Grotevant, Wendy L. Hellerstedt, and Megan R. Gunnar, "Cultural Socialization in Families with Internationally Adopted Children," *Journal of Family Psychology* 20, no. 4 (December 2006): 571–80, https://doi.org/10.1037/0893-3200.20.4.571.

30 Lee et al., "Cultural Socialization in Families," 571–80.

31 Bonilla Silva, *Racism without Racists: Colorblind Racism and the Persistence of Racial Inequality in the United States* (New York, NY: Rowman & Littlefield, 2003).

32 Lee et al., "Cultural Socialization in Families," 571–80."

33 Smith, Juarez, and Jacobson, "Can White Parents Teach Black Adoptive Children?" 1195–230.

34 Pamela Anne Quiroz, "Cultural Tourism in Transnational Adoption: 'Staged Authenticity' and Its Implications for Adopted Children." *Journal of Family Issues* 33, no. 4 (April 2012): 527–55, https://doi.org/10.1177/0192513X11418179.

35 Monica Pellerone, Alessia Passanisi, and Mario Filippo Paolo Bellomo, "Identity Development, Intelligence Structure, and Interests: A Cross-Sectional Study in a Group of Italian Adolescents During the Decision-Making Process," *Psychological Research and Behavioral Management* 8 (August 20, 2015): 239–249, https://doi.org/10.2147/PRBM.S88631.

36 Melissa Guida-Richards, "Abby Johnson's Video Shows the Problem with White Parents Adopting Children of Color," ZORA, Medium, August 28, 2020, https://zora.medium.com/abby-johnsons-video-shows-the-problem-with-white-parents-adopting-children-of-color-949b602e1328.

37 Joshua B. Padilla, Jose H. Vargas, and H. Lyssette Chavez, "Influence of Age on Transracial Foster Adoptions and Its Relation to Ethnic Identity Development," *Adoption Quarterly* 13, no. 1 (April 2, 2010): 50–73, https://doi.org/10.1080/10926751003662598.

38  Padilla, Vargas, and Chavez, "Influence of Age on Transracial Foster Adoptions," 57–73.

39  Raushanah Hud-Aleem and Jacqueline Countryman, "Biracial Identity Development and Recommendations in Therapy," *Psychiatry (Edgmont)* vol. 5, no. 11 (November 2008): 37–44, https://www .ncbi.nlm.nih.gov/pmc/articles/PMC2695719/.

40  Jordan E. Montgomery and Nickolas A. Jordan, "Racial–Ethnic Socialization and Transracial Adoptee Outcomes: A Systematic Research Synthesis," *Child and Adolescent Social Work Journal* 35, no. 5 (2018): 439–58, https://doi.org/10.1007/s10560-018-0541-9.

41  Montgomery and Jordan, "Racial–Ethnic Socialization and Transracial Adoptee Outcomes," 439–58.

42  Janet E. Helms and Robert T. Carter, "Relationships of White and Black Racial Identity Attitudes and Demographic Similarity to Counselor Preferences." *Journal of Counseling Psychology* 38, no. 4 (1991): 446–57, https://doi.org/10.1037/0022-0167.38.4.446.

43  Children's Bureau, "Access to Adoption Records," Child Welfare.gov, accessed February 15, 2021, https://www.childwelfare.gov/pubPDFs /infoaccessap.pdf.

44  Hazel Kelly, "5 Things to Know Before You Take a Home DNA Test," California State University, June 22, 2018, https://www2 .calstate.edu/csu-system/news/Pages/5-Things-to-Know-Home-DNA -Test.aspx.

45  Ellen, Matloff, "If I'm Adopted, Should I Have DNA Testing?" *Forbes*, July 11, 2018, https://www.forbes.com/sites/ellenmatloff /2018/07/11/im-adopted-should-i-have-dna-testing/?sh =4355ade5e029.

46  Sharon Glennen, "Language Development and Delay in Internationally Adopted Infants and Toddlers: A Review," *American Journal of Speech-Language Pathology* 11, no. 4 (November 2002): 333–39, https://doi.org/10.1044/1058-0360(2002/038).

47  Boris Gindis, "Cognitive, Language, and Educational Issues of Children Adopted from Overseas Orphanages," *Journal of Cognitive Education and Psychology* 4, no. 3 (2005): 291–315, https://doi.org /10.1891/194589505787382720.

48  Glennen, "Language Development and Delay," 333–39.

49  Jiyoun Choi, Mirjam Broersma, and Anne Cutler, "Early Phonology Revealed by International Adoptees' Birth Language Retention," *Proceedings of the National Academy of Sciences of the United States of America* 114, no. 28 (2017): 7307–312, https://doi.org/10.1073/pnas.1706405114.

50  Glennen, "Language Development and Delay," 333–39.

51  Gindis, "Cognitive, Language, and Educational Issues," 291–315.

52  Abigail Mouring, "Adopting Heritage: What Influences Adoptive Parents in Heritage Language Decisions for Their Internationally Adopted Children," Linguistics Senior Research Projects, Department of English, Literature and Foreign Languages, Cedarville University (April 26, 2019), 20, https://digitalcommons.cedarville.edu/linguistics_senior_projects/20.

53  Sarah J. Shin, "Transforming Culture and Identity: Transnational Adoptive Families and Heritage Language Learning," *Language, Culture and Curriculum* 26, no.2 (2013): 161–178, https://doi.org/10.1080/07908318.2013.809095.

54  *Dictionary.com*, s.v. "Code-Switching," accessed February 15, 2021, https://www.dictionary.com/browse/code-switching.

55  Kate Stitham, "Code-Switching in the Workplace: Understanding Cultures of Power," Integrative Inquiry, January 7, 2021, https://www.integrativeinquiryllc.com/post/the-problem-with-code-switching-addressing-the-dominant-culture.

56  Courtney McCluney, "The Costs of Code-Switching," *Harvard Business Review*, November 5, 2020, https://hbr.org/2019/11/the-costs-of-codeswitching.

# Chapter 3

1  Jo Jones, "Adoption Experiences of Women and Men and Demand for Children to Adopt by Women 18–44 Years of Age in the United States," *Vital and Health Statistics* 23, no. 27 (August 2008): 1–36.

2  Jo Jones, "Who Adopts? Characteristics of Women and Men Who Have Adopted Children," Centers for Disease Control and Prevention, November 6, 2015, https://www.cdc.gov/nchs/products/databriefs/db12.htm.

3 Theresa Waldrop, "Tennessee Governor Signs Bill Allowing Adoption Agencies to Reject LGBTQ Applicants," CNN: Politics, January 24, 2020, https://www.cnn.com/2020/01/24/politics/tennessee-governor -adoption-foster-care-bill/index.html.

4 Darlene Gerow, "Infant Adoption Is Big Business in America," Origins Canada, accessed February 15, 2021, https://www.originscan-ada.org/documents/infant.pdf.

5 Department of Economic and Social Affairs, *Child Adoption: Trends and Policies* (New York: United Nations, 2009), 1–486, https:// www.un.org/en/development/desa/population/publications/pdf /policy/child-adoption.pdf.

6 Kathryn A Sweeney, "Race-Conscious Adoption Choices, Multira-ciality, and Color-Blind Racial Ideology," *Family Relations: An Inter-disciplinary Journal of Applied Family Studies* 62, no. 1 (February 2013): 42–57, https://doi.org/10.1111/j.1741-3729.2012.00757.x.

7 Michele Goodwin, "The Free-Market Approach to Adoption: The Value of a Baby," *Boston College Third World Law Journal* 26, no. 1 (2006), http://lawdigitalcommons.bc.edu/twlj/vol26/iss1/5.

8 Madeline Engel, Norma Phillips, and Frances Della Cava, "Inter-Country Adoption of Children Born in the United States," *Sociology between the Gaps: Forgotten and Neglected Topics* 1, no. 1 (March 2015), https://digitalcommons.providence.edu/cgi/viewcontent.cgi ?article=1000&context=sbg.

9 *Merriam-Webster.com*, s. v. "colorism," accessed February 15, 2021, https://www.merriam-webster.com/dictionary/colorism.

10 Sweeney, "Race-Conscious Adoption Choices," 42–57.

11 Pamela Anne Quiroz, "Latino and Asian Infant Adoption: From Mongrels to 'Honorary White' or White?" *Journal of Latino-Latin American Studies (JOLLAS)* 2, no. 3 (2007): 46–58, https://doi.org /10.18085/llas.2.3.43qv4p04t4277136.

12 Quiroz, "Latino and Asian Infant Adoption," 46–58.

13 Quiroz, "Latino and Asian Infant Adoption," 46–58.

14 Nicholas Levy, Cindy Harmon-Jones, and Eddie Harmon-Jones, "Dissonance and Discomfort: Does a Simple Cognitive Inconsis-tency Evoke a Negative Affective State?" *Motivation Science* 4, no. 2 (2018): 95–108, https://doi.org/10.1037/mot0000079.

15 Susan Burke, Glen Schmidt, Shannon Wagner, Ross Hoffman, and Neil Hanlon, "Cognitive Dissonance in Social Work," *Journal of Public Child Welfare* 11, no. 3 (February 2017): 299–317, https://doi.org/10.1080/15548732.2016.1278068.

16 Engel, Phillips, and Della Cava, "Inter-Country Adoption in the United States."

17 Department of Economic and Social Affairs, "Child Adoption: Trends and Policies," 1–486.

18 Patricia K Jennings, "The Trouble with the Multiethnic Placement Act: An Empirical Look at Transracial Adoption," *Sociological Perspectives* 49, no. 4 (December 2006): 559–81, https://doi.org/10.1525/sop.2006.49.4.559.

19 Elizabeth Bartholet, "International Adoption, the Human Rights Position," *Global Policy* 1, no. 1 (January 2010): 91–100, https://doi.org/10.1111/j.1758-5899.2009.00001.x.

20 Department of Economic and Social Affairs, "Child Adoption: Trends and Policies," 1–486.

21 Victor Groza and Kelley McCreery Bunkers, "The United States as a Sending Country for Intercountry Adoption: Birth Parents' Rights versus the 1993 Hague Convention on Intercountry Adoption," *Adoption Quarterly* 17, no. 1 (2014): 44–64, http://doi.org/10.1080/10926755.2014.875089.

22 Joan Heifetz Hollinger, "Overview of the Multiethnic Placement Act (MEPA)," Ct.gov, 2006–2007, http://www.ct.gov/ccpa/lib/ccpa/MEPA_(Multi-Ethnic_Placement_Act).pdf.

23 Jennings, "The Trouble with the Multiethnic Placement Act," 559–81.

24 Mary Annette Pember, "Death by Civilization," *The Atlantic,* March 8, 2019, https://www.theatlantic.com/education/archive/2019/03/traumatic-legacy-indian-boarding-schools/584293/.

25 Sheila Hogan, "Child and Family Services," DPHHS, Montana.gov, accessed February 16, 2021, https://dphhs.mt.gov/cfsd/icwa/icwahistory.

26 "Setting the Record Straight: The Indian Child Welfare Act Fact Sheet," National Indian Child Welfare Association, September 2015, https://www.nicwa.org/wp-content/uploads/2017/04/Setting-the-Record-Straight-ICWA-Fact-Sheet.pdf.

27  Leah Litman and Matthew L.M. Fletcher, "The Necessity of the Indian Child Welfare Act," *The Atlantic*, January 22, 2020, https:// www.theatlantic.com/ideas/archive/2020/01/fifth-circuit-icwa /605167/.

28  Travel.State.Gov, "Understanding the Hague Convention," US Department of State: Bureau of Consular Affairs, Accessed February 16, 2021, https://travel.state.gov/content/travel/en/Intercountry -Adoption/Adoption-Process/understanding-the-hague-convention .html.

29  Sweeney, "Race-Conscious Adoption Choices," 42–57.

30  Gina Miranda Samuels, "'Being Raised by White People': Navigating Racial Difference among Adopted Multiracial Adults," *Journal of Marriage and Family* 71, no.1 (January 27, 2009): 80–94, https:// doi.org/10.1111/j.1741-3737.2008.00581.x.

31  Samuels, "Being Raised by White People.," 80-94.

32  Quiroz, "Latino and Asian Infant Adoption," 46–58.

33  Quiroz, "Latino and Asian Infant Adoption," 46–58.

34  Samuels, "Being Raised by White People,"80–94.

35  Samuels, "Being Raised by White People,"80–94.

36  Samuels, "Being Raised by White People," 80–94.

37  Sophie Brown, "Overseas Adoptions Rise—for Black American Children," CNN, September 17, 2013, http://www.cnn.com/2013/09/16 /world/international-adoption-us-children-adopted-abroad/.

38  Brown, "Overseas Adoptions Rise."

39  Don Lash, "Race and Class in the US Foster Care System," *International Socialist Review* 91, Winter 2013–14, https://isreview.org /issue/91/race-and-class-us-foster-care-system.

40  Joshua B. Padilla, Jose H. Vargas, and H. Lyssette Chavez, "Influence of Age on Transracial Foster Adoptions and Its Relation to Ethnic Identity Development," *Adoption Quarterly* 13, no. 1 (2010): 50–73, https://doi.org/10.1080/10926751003662598.

41  Padilla, Vargas, and Chavez, Influence of Age on Transracial Foster Adoptions," 50–73.

42  Padilla, Vargas, and Chavez, Influence of Age on Transracial Foster Adoptions," 50–73.

43  Chibnall, Susan. "Children of Color in the Child Welfare System: Perspectives from the Child Welfare Community," Howard

University School of Social Work, December 2003, https://www
.childwelfare.gov/pubpdfs/children.pdf.

44 Malika Saar, Rebecca Epstein, Lindsay Rosenthal, and Yasmin Vafa,
*The Sexual Abuse to Prison Pipeline: The Girls' Story*, Human Rights
Project for Girls (Washington, DC: Center on Poverty and Equality
/Georgetown Law, February 10, 2018), https://rights4girls.org/wp
-content/uploads/2020/11/SexualAbusetoPrisonPipeline-Report.pdf.

45 Marianne Bitler and Madeline Zavodny, "Did Abortion Legalization
Reduce the Number of Unwanted Children? Evidence from Adop-
tions," *Perspectives on Sexual Reproduction and Health* 34, no. 1
(January/February 2003): 25-33.

46 Jo Jones, "Adoption Experiences of Women and Men," 1–36.

47 Gretchen Sisson, Lauren Ralph, Heather Gould, and Diana Gree
Foster, "Adoption Decision Making among Women Seeking Abortion," *Women's Health Issues* 27, no. 2 (March/April 2017): 136–144,
https://doi.org/10.1016/j.whi.2016.11.007.

48 Melissa Guida-Richards, (@adoptee_thoughts), Instagram photo
and caption, November 23, 2020, https://www.instagram.com/p
/CH88R34BpN7/.

49 CNA, "Pro-Adoption Ad Campaign Reaches Women Nationwide,"
Catholic News Agency, January 9, 2013, https://www.catholicnews
agency.com/news/pro-adoption-ad-campaign-reaches-women
-nationwide.

50 Children's Bureau, "Use of Advertising and Facilitators in Adoptive Placements," ChildWelfare.gov/US Department of Health and
Human Services, accessed February 16, 2021, https://www.child
welfare.gov/pubpdfs/advertising.pdf.

51 @lisa_furmana, Twitter, March 31, 2020.

52 @Tamcolady (Marlene Labelle) Twitter, April 1, 2020, 5:42 p.m.,
https://twitter.com/Tamcolady/status/1284399259996106752?s=20.

53 @Jennie_Sims4117 (Jennie), Twitter, March 31,
2020, 1:04 p.m., https://twitter.com/Jennie_Sims17/
status/1245034208306724865?s=20.

54 Jamilah Lemieux, "Dear Care and Feeding: I Don't Think My Niece
Is Ready for a Baby. Should I Take the Child?" *Slate*, July 22, 2020,
https://slate.com/human-interest/2020/07/adopting-nieces-baby-care
-and-feeding.html.

55  *Cambridge English Dictionary Online*, s.v. "individualism," accessed August 2, 2020, https://dictionary.cambridge.org/us/dictionary /english/individualism.

56  Olusesan Ayodeji Makinde, "Infant Trafficking and Baby Factories: A New Tale of Child Abuse in Nigeria," *Child Abuse Review* 25, 6 (November/December 2016): 433–43, https://doi.org/10.1002 /car.2420.

57  OHCHR, "Illegal Adoptions," United Nations Office of the High Commissioner Human Rights, accessed February 18, 2021, https:// www.ohchr.org/EN/Issues/Children/Pages/Illegaladoptions.aspx.

58  Lindsay Whitehurst, "Paul Petersen Pleads Guilty to Human Smuggling in Adoption Scheme," FOX 10 Phoenix, June 19, 2020, https:// www.fox10phoenix.com/news/paul-petersen-pleads-guilty-to-human-smuggling-in-adoption-scheme.

59  Jessica Boehm and Robert Anglen, "'A Baby-Selling Enterprise': Former Arizona Elected Official Sentenced to 6-Plus Years in Adoption Scheme," *USA Today*, December 2, 2020, https://www.usatoday .com/story/news/nation/2020/12/01/paul-petersen-sentenced-6-plus -years-adoption-scheme/3786156001/.

60  Robert Anglen, "Latter-day Saints Apostle Ronald Rasband Calls Paul Petersen's Adoption Scheme 'Sickening,'" *The Arizona Republic*, November 11, 2019, https://www.azcentral.com/story/news/local /arizona-investigations/2019/11/10/latter-day-saints-mormon-apostle -ronald-rasband-calls-paul-petersens-adoption-scheme-sickening /4156526002/.

61  Lily Altavena, Jessica Boehm, and Uriel J. Garcia, "'Purest Form of Human Trafficking': Arizona Official Indicted in Adoption Fraud Scheme," *USA Today*, October 10, 2019, https://www.usatoday.com /story/news/nation/2019/10/09/paul-petersen-arizona-official -indicted-adoption-fraud-scheme/3926733002/.

62  Teo Armus and Maria Sacchetti, "The Parents of 545 Children Separated at the Border Still Haven't Been Found. The Pandemic Isn't Helping," *Washington Post*, October 22, 2020, https://www .washingtonpost.com/nation/2020/10/21/family-separation -parents-border-covid/.

63  The Associated Press, "Deported Parents May Lose Kids to Adoption, Investigation Finds," NBCNews.com, October 10, 2018,

https://www.nbcnews.com/news/latino/deported-parents-may-lose
-kids-adoption-investigation-finds-n918261.

64  The Associated Press, "Deported Parents May Lose Kids to Adoption."

65  Ann Fessler, *The Girls Who Went Away: The Hidden History of
Women Who Surrendered Children for Adoption in the Decades
before Roe v. Wade* (New York: Penguin Press, 2007).

66  Jana Shortal, "Finding Christopher: One Mother's Story from the
'Baby Scoop Era,'" kare11.com, November 12, 2018, https://www
.kare11.com/article/news/finding-christopher-one-mothers-story
-from-the-baby-scoop-era/89-522607040.

67  Rachel Martin and NPR Staff, "Remembering the Doomed First
Flight of Operation Babylift," NPR, April 26, 2015, https://www
.npr.org/2015/04/26/402208267/remembering-the-doomed-first
-flight-of-operation-babylift.

68  PBS, "Daughter from Danang: Operation Babylift (1975)," PBS:
American Experience, accessed February 18, 2021, https://www.pbs
.org/wgbh/americanexperience/features/daughter-operation-babylift
-1975/.

69  PBS, "Daughter from Danang."

70  Makinde, "Infant Trafficking and Baby Factories,"433–43.

71  Jodie Fleischer, Rick Yarborough, and Steve Jones, "Tens of Thousands of Adoptees Learn They Aren't US Citizens, Even After
Decades Living Here," NBC4 Washington, February 4, 2019, https://
www.nbcwashington.com/news/local/tens-of-thousands-of-adoptees
-learn-they-arent-us-citizens-even-after-decades-living-here/3297/.

72  US Citizenship and Immigration Services, "U.S. Citizenship for an
Adopted Child." USCIS.gov, November 18, 2020, https://www.uscis
.gov/adoption/bringing-your-internationally-adopted-child-to-the
-united-states/us-citizenship-for-an-adopted-child.

73  Marisa Kwiatkowski, "'You Love This Country, and It's Taken from
You': Adoption Doesn't Guarantee US Citizenship." USA Today. Gan-
nett Satellite Information Network, December 16, 2020. https://www
.usatoday.com/in-depth/news/investigations/2020/12/16/international
-adoption-does-not-guarantee-adoptees-us-citizenship/6310358002/.

74  Anissa Dreusedow, interview by Melissa Guida-Richards, *Adoptee
Thoughts*, July, 2020, https://podcasts.apple.com/us/podcast/adoptee
-thoughts/id1514056644?i=1000486123122.

75  Dreusedow, interview by Guida-Richards.

76  Adoptees for Justice, "The Adoptee Citizenship Act: Current Status," accessed February 18, 2020, https://adopteesforjustice.org /adopteecitizenship/.

77  Adoptees for Justice, "Adoptee Citizenship Act."

78  Pamela Anne Quiroz, "Cultural Tourism in Transnational Adoption: 'Staged Authenticity' and Its Implications for Adopted Children," *Journal of Family Issues*, September 25, 2011, https://doi.org/10 .1177/0192513X11418179.

79  Gerow, "Infant Adoption Is Big Business."

80  American Adoptions, "How to Complete the Home Study: 4 Steps of the Adoption Home Study Process," AmericanAdoptions.com, accessed February 18, 2020, https://www.americanadoptions.com /adopt/home_study.

81  Children's Bureau, "Planning for Adoption: Knowing the Costs and Resources," Child Welfare Information Gateway, accessed February 18, 2021, https://www.childwelfare.gov/pubPDFs/s_costs.pdf.

82  Children's Bureau, "Adoption Assistance for Children Adopted from Foster Care," Child Welfare Information Gateway, June 2020, https://www.childwelfare.gov/pubPDFs/f_subsid.pdf.

83  Children's Bureau, "Intercountry Adoption from Hague Convention and Non-Hague Convention Countries," Child Welfare Information Gateway, 2014, https://www.childwelfare.gov/pubPDFs/hague.pdf.

84  Elizabeth Raleigh, "Conclusion: The Consequences of Selling Transracial Adoption and the Implications for Adoptive Families," In *Selling Transracial Adoption: Families, Markets, and the Color Line* (Philadelphia: Temple University Press, 2018), 190–202, https://doi.org/10.2307/j.ctt21216x4.10.

85  Raleigh, "Consequences of Selling Transracial Adoption," 190–202.

86  "Supply and Demand, Markets and Prices," The Library of Economics and Liberty, accessed February 18, 2021, https://www.econlib .org/library/Topics/College/supplyanddemand.html.

87  AdoptUSKids, "What Is the Cost of Adoption from Foster Care?" AdoptUSKids.org, accessed February 18, 2021, https://www.adopt uskids.org/adoption-and-foster-care/overview/what-does-it -cost.

# Chapter 4

1  CDC, "Racial and Ethnic Disparities Continue in Pregnancy-Related Deaths," Centers for Disease Control and Prevention, September 6, 2019, https://www.cdc.gov/media/releases/2019/p0905-racial-ethnic -disparities-pregnancy-deaths.html.

2  Children's Bureau, "Unregulated Custody Transfer of Adopted Children," US Department of Health and Human Services, Administration for Children and Families, August 2019, https://www .childwelfare.gov/news-events/adoptiontriad/editions/aug2019/.

3  Margot Harris, "A Parenting YouTuber Faced Backlash for 'Rehoming' Her Adopted Son with Autism after Monetizing His Videos. This Is How the Story Unfolded," *Insider*, June 1, 2020, https:// www.insider.com/myka-stauffer-huxley-parenting-youtube-rehome -adopted-son-timeline-2020-5.

4  Children's Bureau, "Adoption Disruption and Dissolution," Child Welfare Information Gateway, ChildWelfare.gov, June 2012, https:// www.childwelfare.gov/pubPDFs/s_disrup.pdf.

5  Rachelle Bergstein, "Parents Who Used Instagram to Adopt a Baby," *New York Post*, July 3, 2018, https://nypost.com/2018/07/03/we -used-instagram-to-adopt-our-baby/.

6  Joseph Driscoll, "Creating Engagement," First Steps Blog, Accessed April 2, 2016, http://www.firststepsadv.com/First_Steps_Advertising _for_Adoption/Welcome/Welcome.html.

7  American Adoptions, "30 Reasons Why Women 'Give a Child Up' for Adoption," americanadoptions.com, February 20, 2021, https:// www.americanadoptions.com/pregnant/reasons-to-give-your-child -up-for-adoption.

8  Regine Cabato and Kayla Epstein, "An American Woman Tried to Leave the Philippines with a Baby in Her Carry-On, Authorities Say," *The Washington Post*, September 4, 2019, https://www .washingtonpost.com/world/2019/09/04/an-american-woman-tried -leave-philippines-with-baby-her-carry-on-authorities-say/.

9  Karen Ruiz and Laura Collins, "Utah Mom Who 'Tried to Smuggle Filipino Newborn on Plane' Posted Ads for Adoption ONLINE Claiming Her Other Kids Attended Private School and Went to 'Church on Sundays,'" DailyMail.com, September 16, 2019,

https://www.dailymail.co.uk/news/article-7457533/Jennifer-Talbot
-posted-ads-adoption-months-trying-smuggle-baby-Philippines.html.

10  NWA, "Weekly WIC Policy Update," National WIC Association,
accessed February 2020, https://www.nwica.org/blog/weekly-wic
-policy-update-185; Dottie Rosenbaum and Zoë Neuberger, "President's 2021 Budget Would Cut Food Assistance for Millions and
Radically Restructure SNAP," Center on Budget and Policy Priorities, February 18, 2020, https://www.cbpp.org/research/food
-assistance/presidents-2021-budget-would-cut-food-assistance-for
-millions-and-radically.

11  Margaret A. Keyes, Stephen M. Malone, Anu Sharma, William G.
Iacono, and Matt McGue, "Risk of Suicide Attempt in Adopted
and Nonadopted Offspring," *Pediatrics* 132, no. 4 (2013): 639–46,
https://doi.org/10.1542/peds.2012-3251.

12  Crystal Walsh-Mungo, Facebook comment in Adoptive Parents
Support, July 1, 2020, https://www.facebook.com/groups
/1194469637352034/permalink/2038144102984579.

13  Jen C, Facebook comment in Adoptive Parents Support, July 1,
2020. https://www.facebook.com/groups/1194469637352034
/permalink/2038144102984579.

14  The Reylo Mother Nerd @NerdMomMusings, Twitter thread,
accessed August 19, 2020, https://twitter.com/NerdMomMusings
/status/1296118821506494466?s=20.

15  Christine D. Bentley, Facebook comment, October 26, 2020, https://
www.facebook.com/groups/TransracialAdoption/permalink
/4547951651943903.

16  Susannah Snider, "Here's How to Pay for Adoption Costs," *U.S.
News & World Report*, June 11, 2020, https://money.usnews.com
/money/personal-finance/family-finance/articles/what-adoption
-costs-and-strategies-to-pay-for-it.

17  Aliyah Santos, interview by author, *Adoptee Thoughts*, August 2020,
https://podcasts.apple.com/us/podcast/interview-with-aliyah-santos
-a-mixed-race-domestic-adoptee/id1514056644?i=1000487770145.

18  Family Youth and Services, "Maternity Group Homes for Pregnant
and Parenting Youth," US Department of Health and Human Services: Administration for Children and Families, accessed February

20, 2021, https://www.acf.hhs.gov/fysb/programs
/runaway-homeless-youth/programs/maternity-group-homes.

19 Family and Youth Services Bureau, "Maternity Group Homes Fact
Sheet," US Department of Health and Human Services: Administration for Children and Families, September 2020, https://www.acf
.hhs.gov/sites/default/files/documents/fysb/mgh_fact_sheet
_september_2020.pdf.

20 Unplanned Pregnancy, "What Are Maternity Homes and Where
Can I Find Them?" UnplannedPregnancy.com, accessed February
20, 2021, https://unplannedpregnancy.com/facing-an-unplanned
-pregnancy/resources/maternity-homes/.

21 Lifeway Research, "Adoption, Foster Care Commonplace in
Churches," Lifeway Christian Resources, January 24, 2018, https://
lifewayresearch.com/2018/01/24/adoption-foster-care-commonplace
-in-churches/.

22 David M. Smolin, "Of Orphans and Adoption, Parents and the Poor
Exploitation and Rescue: A Scriptural and Theological Critique of
the Evangelical Christian Adoption and Orphan Care Movement,"
*Regent Journal of International Law* 8, no. 2 (Spring 2012), http://
works.bepress.com/david_smolin/10/.

23 Traci Cline, "Adoption and the Church: The Good, the Bad, and the
Beautiful," Western North Carolina Conference, United Methodist
Church, October 2015, https://www.wnccumc.org/adoption-and
-the-church-the-good-the-bad-and-the-beautiful.

24 Melissa Guida-Richards, "I Was Adopted Outside of the US and
Have Disabilities. I'm Tired of the Savior Narrative among White
Adoptive Parents," *Insider*, June 3, 2020, https://www.insider.com
/im-an-adoptee-im-tired-white-saviors-like-myka-stauffer-2020-6.

25 Kathryn Joyce, "The Trouble with the Christian Adoption Movement," *The New Republic*, January 11, 2016, https://newrepublic
.com/article/127311/trouble-christian-adoption-movement.

# Chapter 5

1 Sydney K. Morgan, and Kimberly J. Langrehr, "Transracially
Adoptive Parents' Colorblindness and Discrimination Recognition:

Adoption Stigma as Moderator," *Cultural Diversity and Ethnic Minority Psychology* 25, no. 2 (2019): 242–52, https://doi.org /10.1037/cdp0000219.

2  Louise Shepherd, interview by Melissa Guida-Richards, *Adoptee Thoughts*, October 2020, https://podcasts.apple.com/us/podcast /adoptee-thoughts/id1514056644?i=1000495111536.

3  Lauren J. Sharkey, interview by Melissa Guida-Richards, *Adoptee Thoughts*, July 2020, https://podcasts.apple.com/us/podcast /adoptee-thoughts/id1514056644?i=1000486743646.

4  Kylie Peterson, interview by Melissa Guida-Richards, *Adoptee Thoughts*, June 2020, https://podcasts.apple.com/us/podcast /adoptee-thoughts/id1514056644?i=1000480858739.

5  "Resilience." Center on the Developing Child at Harvard University, August 17, 2020, https://developingchild.harvard.edu/science /key-concepts/resilience/.

6  Anders Hjern, Frank Lindblad, and Bo Vinnerljung, "Suicide, Psychiatric Illness, and Social Maladjustment in Intercountry Adoptees in Sweden: A Cohort Study," *The Lancet* 360, no. 9331 (2002): 443–48, https://doi.org/10.1016/S0140-6736(02)09674-5.

7  Patricia Lantis, "We Don't Know What We Don't Know: Post Adoption Support of Families Caring for Traumatized Children," *Journal of Applied Research on Children: Informing Policy for Children at Risk* 9, no. 1, Article 6. (2018), https://digitalcommons.library.tmc .edu/childrenatrisk/vol9/iss1/6.

8  Richard M. Lee, "The Transracial Adoption Paradox: History, Research, and Counseling Implications of Cultural Socialization," *The Counseling Psychologist* 31, no. 6 (2003): 711–744, https://doi.org/10.1177/0011000003258087.

9  Jessica Luciere, "An Interview with Jessica Luciere, Colombian Adoptee and Mentorship Director,'" *Adoptee Thoughts*, July 2020, https://podcasts.apple.com/us/podcast/adoptee-thoughts/id15140566 44?i=1000485110590.

# Chapter 6

1  Department of Economic and Social Affairs, "Child Adoption: Trends and Policies," United Nations, 2009, https://www.un.org

/en/development/desa/population/publications/pdf/policy/child
-adoption.pdf.

# Chapter 7

1  Melissa Guida-Richards, @guidarichards, Twitter thread, August 21,
   2020, https://twitter.com/GuidaRichards/status/1296894237569671
   180?s=20.

# Chapter 9

1  Lauren J. Sharkey, "An Interview with Lauren Sharkey, Adoptee and
   Author of 'Inconvenient Daughter,'" *Adoptee Thoughts*, July 2020,
   https://podcasts.apple.com/us/podcast/interview-lauren-sharkey
   -adoptee-author-inconvenient/id1514056644?i=1000486743646.
2  Anonymous Instagram question by @adoptee_thoughts, on August
   9, 2020, https://www.instagram.com/adoptee_thoughts/.
3  Children's Bureau, "Finding and Working with Adoption-Competent
   Therapists," US Department of Health and Human Services, November 2018, https://www.childwelfare.gov/pubPDFs/f_therapist.pdf.
4  Anika E. Behle, and Martin Pinquart, "Psychiatric Disorders and
   Treatment in Adoptees: A Meta-Analytic Comparison with Non-
   Adoptees," *Adoption Quarterly* 19, no. 4 (July 13, 2016): 284–306,
   https://doi.org/10.1080/10926755.2016.1201708.
5  Lisa Rapp-Paglicci, Chris Stewart, and William Rowe, "Improving
   Outcomes for At-Risk Youth: Findings from the Prodigy Cultural
   Arts Program," *Journal of Evidence-Based Social Work* 9, no. 5
   (2012): 512–23, https://doi.org/10.1080/15433714.2011.581532.
6  Anonymous response by adoptive parent to a Google survey conducted by author, May 20, 2020.
7  Anonymous response by adoptive parent to a Google survey conducted by the author, June 2020.
8  Marietta E. Spencer, "The Terminology of Adoption." *Child Welfare*
   58, no. 7 (July–August 1979): 451–459.
9  Karen Buterbaugh, "Whitewashing Adoption: A Critique of 'Respectful Adoption Language,'" SSRN, January 2, 2013, https://ssrn.com
   /abstract=2195774 or http://dx.doi.org/10.2139/ssrn.2195774.

10 TTami, @1966adoptee, Twitter thread, June 23, 2020, https://twitter.com/1966adoptee/status/1275550673707253760?s=21.

11 Anonymous response by adoptive parent to survey conducted by the author, May 20, 2020.

12 TTami, "Adoptees: Which Adoption Term Are You Most Triggered by and Want to See It Gone?" Twitter thread, June 23, 2020, @ttcckk66 https://twitter.com/ttcckk66/status/1275550673707253760?s=20.

# INDEX

# ACKNOWLEDGMENTS

First and foremost, I would like to thank my husband, Charles Richards II, for believing in this book before I even understood what it needed to be. Your belief in me keeps me going every day.

Next, I have to thank my parents, for loving me and for doing the work to help make our relationship stronger. It takes a lot of courage and strength to be open to learning about tough topics like racism, and I want everyone to know how important you both were for inspiring me. Especially, my dear mother who listened to me every step of the way, despite her initial reservations. You are my greatest supporter. Love you, Mom.

To my birth family, I love each and every one of you and am so glad we have reconnected. Having you all in my life has been more special than I could ever put into words.

To Danielle Renino, my wonderful critique partner and friend. You are my rock and my constant inspiration. I can't wait to see what else we can accomplish with the support of one another.

Next, I want to thank my new and beautiful friend, Lauren Sharkey. You will never understand how amazing you are. Thank you both for talking me through my anxieties and for believing in my work when I had my doubts.

I also send endless thanks to my brilliant agent Tina Wainscott. To work with an adoptive parent who believes in my vision has been beyond helpful. Endless thanks to the rest of the Seymour Agency family for all your support as well.

To Shayna Keyles my brilliant editor who saw promise in my idea from my first few posts on Twitter. Your insight and passion have helped me shape this book into what it is today. Thank you for working with me past that initial phone call and for believing in my book when I decided to completely overhaul it and take it in a new direction. Thank you to Janelle, Emily, and the rest of the wonderful staff at North Atlantic Books who supported my book in a thousand different ways.

To the adoptive parents who stood with me during this process—your support has been invaluable. Terra Castro, Brittany Salmon, you two have been such great cheerleaders and I am glad to call you my friends.

And lastly, a huge shout-out to the entire adoption community, especially Stephanie Oyler, Sandhya Oaks, and Lanise Shelley. Your support means the world.

# ABOUT THE AUTHOR

PHOTO CREDIT: CHARLES RICHARDS II

Melissa Guida-Richards is an author, adoptee, and advocate based in Pennsylvania. She was adopted in 1993 from Bogotá, Colombia, to a family in the US. Her viral essay, "My Adoptive Parents Hid My Racial Identity from Me for 19 Years," was published on HuffPost in April 2019. Shortly after, she launched the *Adoptee Thoughts* Instagram and podcast to help elevate adoptee voices and educate adoptive parents on the nuances and complexity of adoption.

Guida-Richards graduated from State University of New York (SUNY) Fredonia in 2015 with a BA in psychology and criminal justice. She published her first book, *Bedtime, the Ultimate Battle: A Parent's Sleep Guide for Infants and Toddlers*, in January of 2020. She has written essays for HuffPost, Zora by Medium, Electric Lit, Embrace Race, and more; she was interviewed by BBC Radio 4 and podcasts such as NPR's *Code Switch*, *Strange Fruit*, and *Do the Work*. She has also appeared on panels, such as the *We the Experts*: Adoptee Speaker Series and is a contributing writer at The Everymom.

You can follow Melissa on Instagram @adoptee_thoughts, listen to her podcast at AdopteeThoughts.com (or any podcast platform), and find all of her work at Guida-Richards.com.

# *About North Atlantic Books*

North Atlantic Books (NAB) is a 501(c)(3) nonprofit publisher committed to a bold exploration of the relationships between mind, body, spirit, culture, and nature. Founded in 1974, NAB aims to nurture a holistic view of the arts, sciences, humanities, and healing. To make a donation or to learn more about our books, authors, events, and newsletter, please visit www.northatlanticbooks.com.